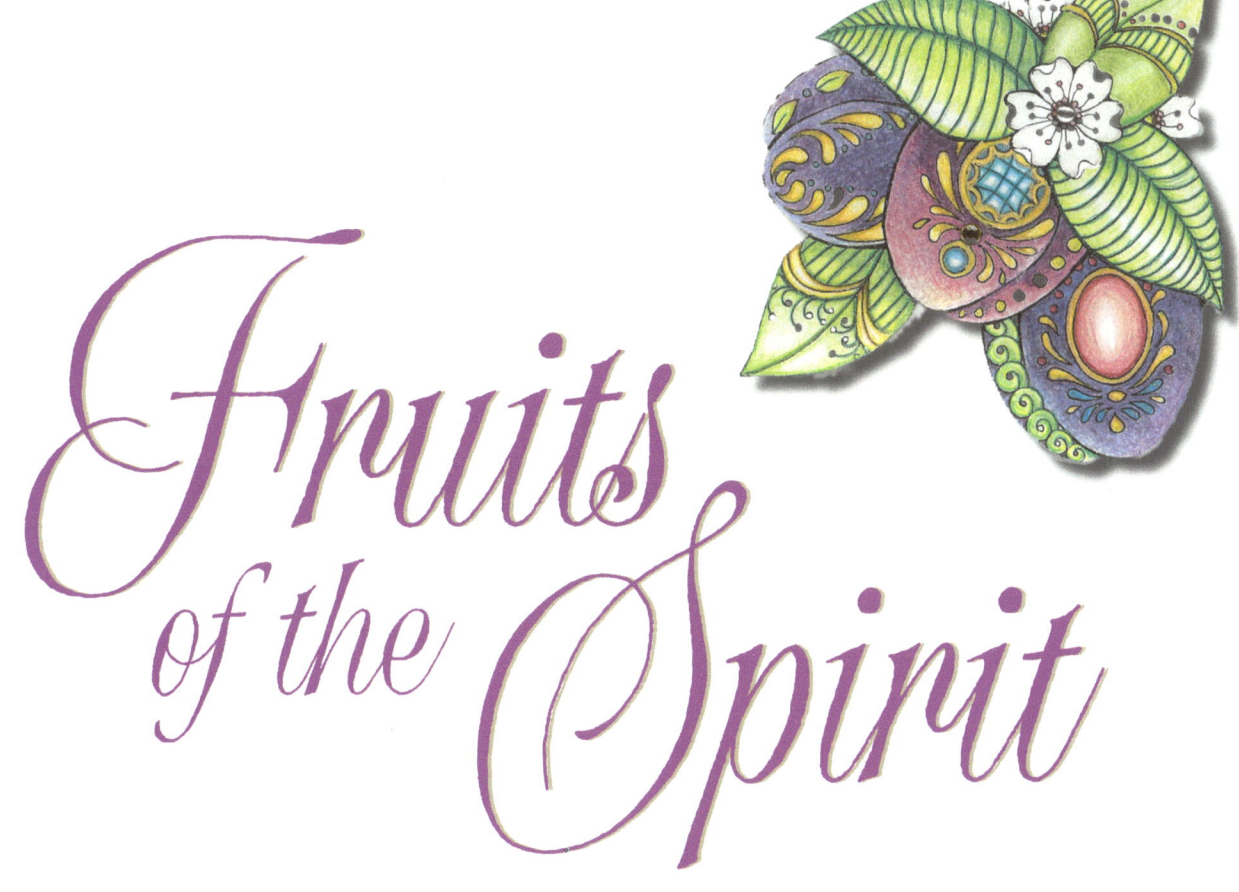

Fruits of the Spirit

Activity Book for Grown Ups
Color + Cut + Embellish

Sherry Crocker

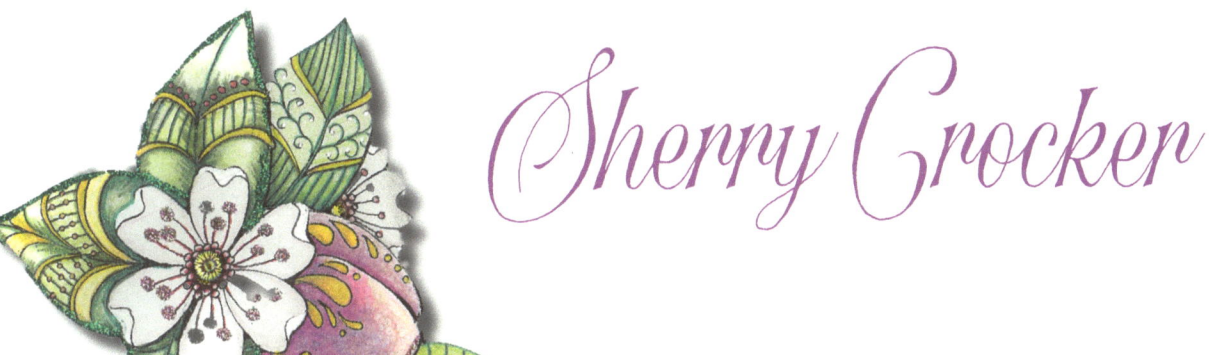

Mission Point Press

Copyright © 2017 by Sherry Crocker
All world rights reserved.

Readers are encouraged to go to www.MissionPointPress.com to contact the author or to find information on how to buy this book in bulk at a discounted rate.

Published by Mission Point Press
2554 Chandler Lake Rd.
Traverse City, MI 49686
(231) 421-9513
www.MissionPointPress.com

ISBN: 978-1-943995-47-9

Printed in the United States of America.

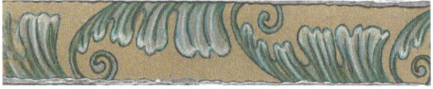

DEDICATION:

always first to my grandparents
Alfred & Olive

&

my Dad who finally got it

SPECIAL THANKS:

Taressa Babcock, without whom this endeavor would be absolutely impossible.

Michelle Ward and David Gerbstadt, for their examples and inspiration to make art a priority.

Patrice Popp Korson, for that first round of technical assistance.

Christine Schneider, whose friendship and entrepreneurial project in Germany provided some friendly and helpful competition (unbeknown to her).

&

All the small voices through the years that have helped me keep my head up in a sea of negativity. You guys really did make a difference.

CONTACT:

A.O.G.Studios, Traverse City,
on Facebook

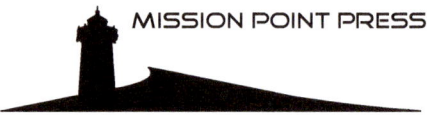

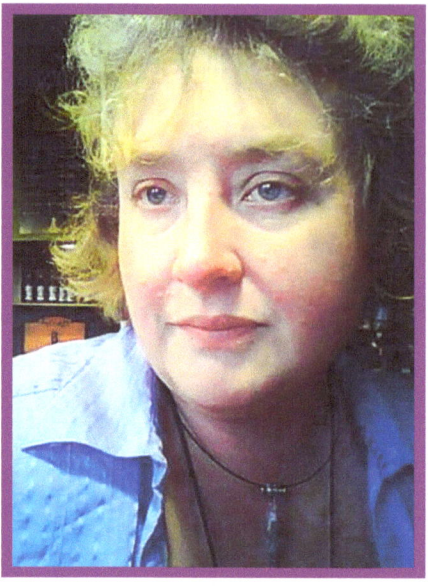

ABOUT THE AUTHOR

As a Traverse City native and former rubber stamp designer, Sherry eats, breathes, and lives art, having tried her hand at almost every artistic medium there is. When she isn't making art for her A.O.G. StudioS endeavor, she explores mediums, researches her special interests (read that as lusts over the visually stunning on Pintrest), collects fonts (oh the fonts!), and drools over visual arts for inspiration and soul cleansing. Music, coffee, chocolate, and Verdigris (Verdi) the art kitty are her constant studio companions.

"All of the fruits (yes, they are all fruits) in this book are inspired by a collection of Styrofoam™ pear ornaments my mother made before becoming a housewife," says Sherry. "Dresden lace, gold foil medallions, sequins, ribbon, faux gemstones and pearls imitated Fabergé eggs. The eggs decorated our holiday tables for many years. As we grew older, and my mother became an art instructor at our school, she created many simple kindergarten projects that became elaborate gifts for our parents—they also tested our finest of fine motor skills and left with me with the habitual desire to make rather than buy. (Although, I am a sucker for a good German hand-blown glass ornament.)"

As a rubber stamp designer and artist, the same principle of "make rather than buy" inspired not only the designs for the stamps themselves, but the projects that we made with them, the likes of which you see on the back cover of this book.

After painstaking sketching—and much erasing—each hand-drawn illustration is inked with Micron pens on Canson art paper before being submitted to the book designer, who then presents them to you to color, cut and embellish. You can use them for card making, scrapbook pages, framed art to use in conjunction with your own rubber stamps, and as holiday or party decorations... anything you can imagine, really.

The pages from this book may NOT be copied for resale or transferred into other mediums. Nor may they be used in commercial sales of handmade or digital art projects without express written permission from the author.

GENERAL INSTRUCTIONS:

You can always leave the pages in the book to color for fun and relaxation.

You also have the option of copying the pages on to your choice of text weight paper or card stock to use in a variety of projects. Simply Copy • Color • Cut • Embellish. Then, incorporate the elements from the "Fruits of the Spirit" into your projects.

Remember to protect your projects during mailing by shipping in a bubble envelope or by covering your embellishments with a piece of scrap card stock.

PLUM ORNAMENT (back cover, illustration 14)

Makes 2 single or 1 double-sided ornament.

- Copy onto a good card stock of your choice.
- Color and cut out.
- Embellish: gemstones, faux pearls, 3D paint, glitter, glitter pens, and crystal lacquer are just a few things you can use to enhance your projects.

For singles:

- Use pop dots or double stick tape to mount the single blossoms over the blossom on the corresponding fruit.
- Attach a ribbon to hang on the backside of the fruit.

For doubles:

- After mounting the single blossoms onto the fruit blossoms, fit your completed fruits together back to back.
- Sandwich a ribbon in between for hanging between your finished pieces.

FIG WREATH (back cover, illustration 11)

2-3 copies makes one wreath.

- Copy image 2-3 times on your choice of card stock.
- Color one sheet completely to use as the base of your project.
- Color only the parts of the second sheet that you wish to stand out from the base—the whole of the top three figs for example.
- From the third sheet, color only the center parts of the top three figs.
- Embellish each layer as you wish.
- Stack the layers using pop dots or double stick tape, being careful to layer them neatly over the corresponding space on the design.

QUARTETS (back cover, illustrations 22, 39,)

Make 4 card fronts or 4 blocking elements for scrapbook pages

- Copy onto your choice of paper or card stock.
- Color, cut, embellish.
- Incorporate into your projects.

STRIPS (illustration 41)

Makes bookmarks, borders for cards and pages, paper chains.

- Copy
- Color, cut embellish

For Bookmarks:

- Mount your colored piece onto a bookmark blank with strong adhesive.
- Or, trim the top of your strip with decorative edged scissors or a paper punch.
- Punch a hole in the top and thread ribbon or yarn through the hole.

For Paper Chains:

Copy onto a heavier text weight paper.

- Color and embellish.
- Cut strips apart and then in half.
- Cut strips from plain, colored or pre-printed text weight paper to the same size as your Fruit pieces.
- Glue the ends of the pieces together, alternating between hand colored and plain links.

ILLUSTRATION 1

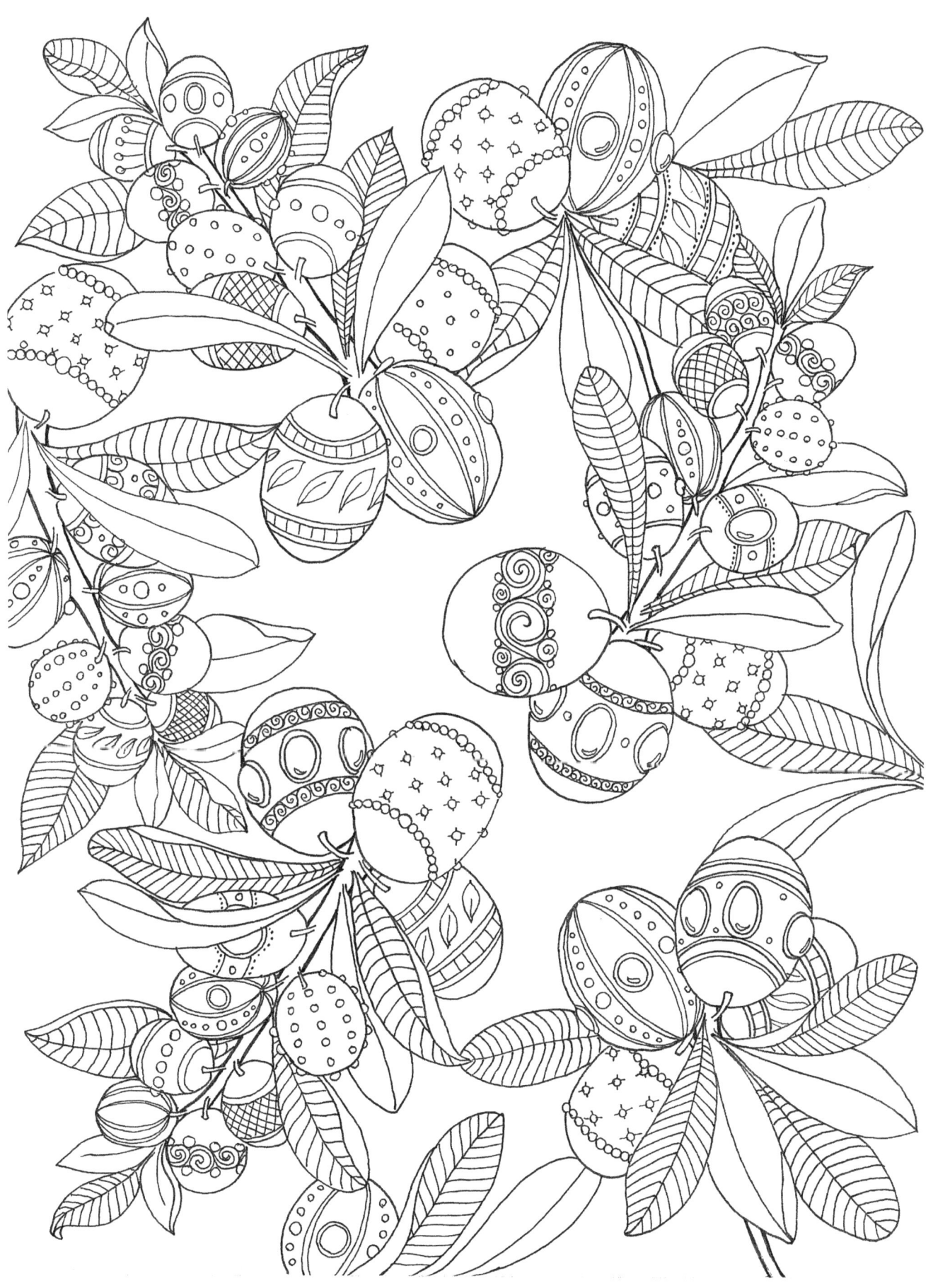

ILLUSTRATION 2

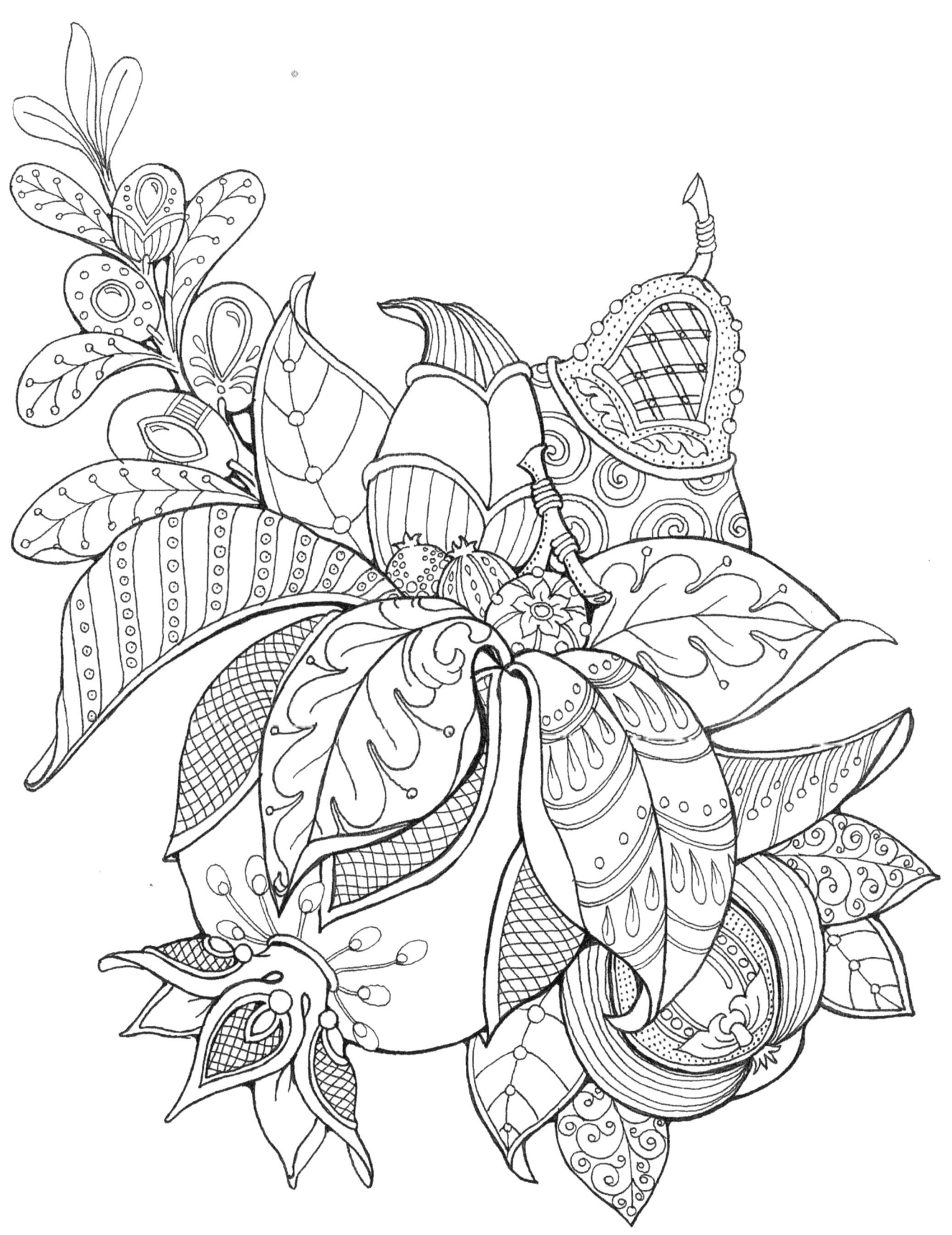

ILLUSTRATION 3

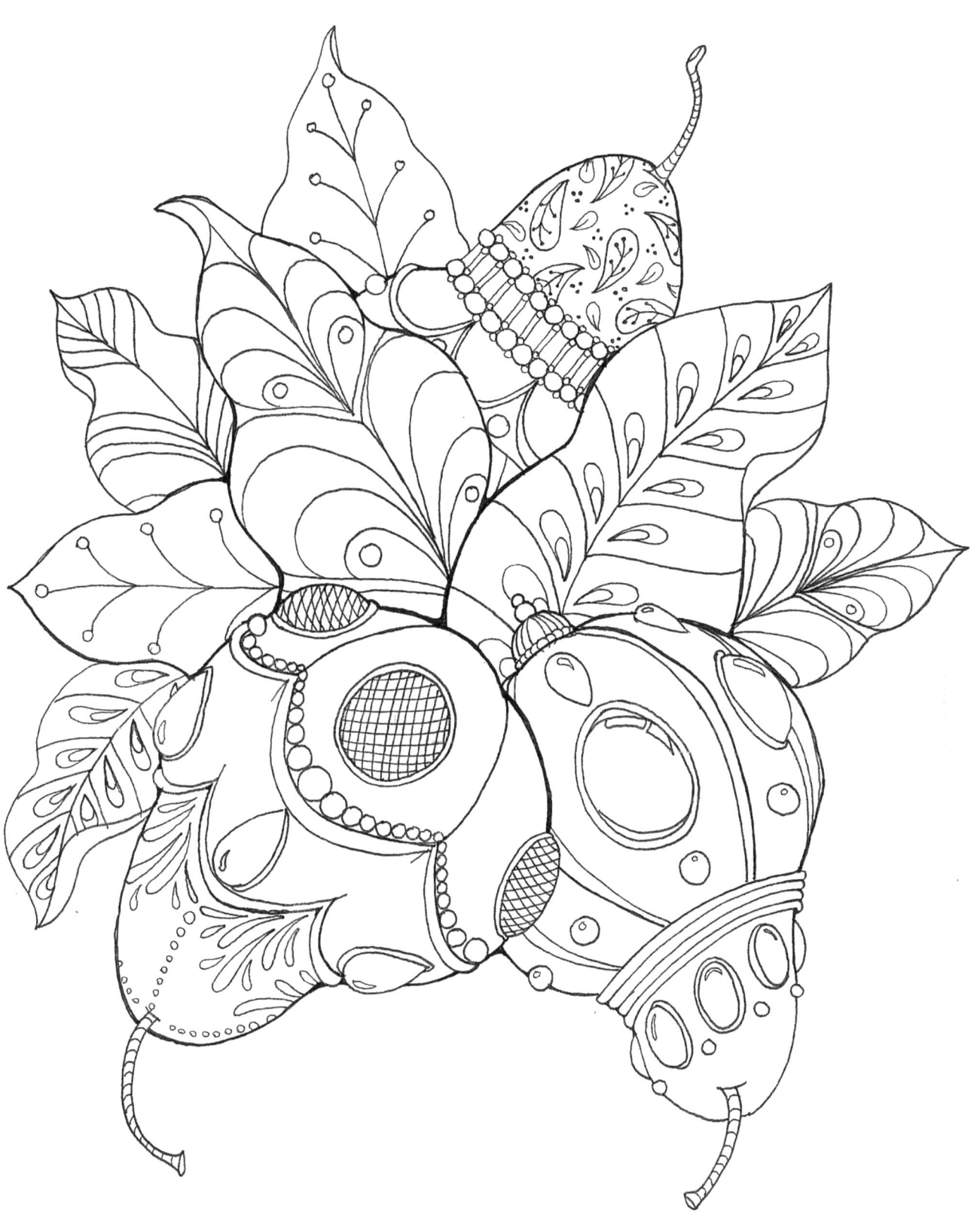

ILLUSTRATION 4

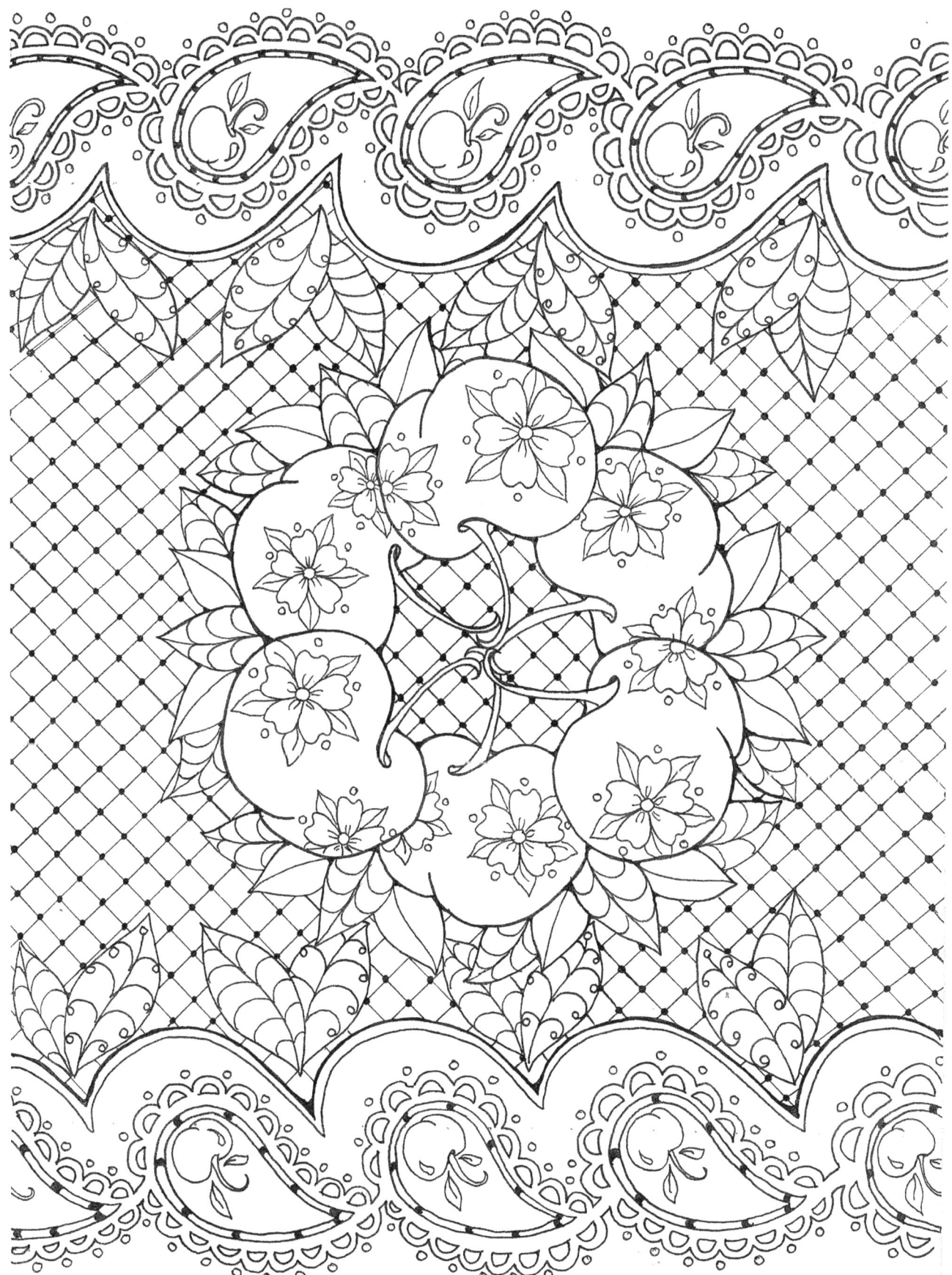

ILLUSTRATION 5

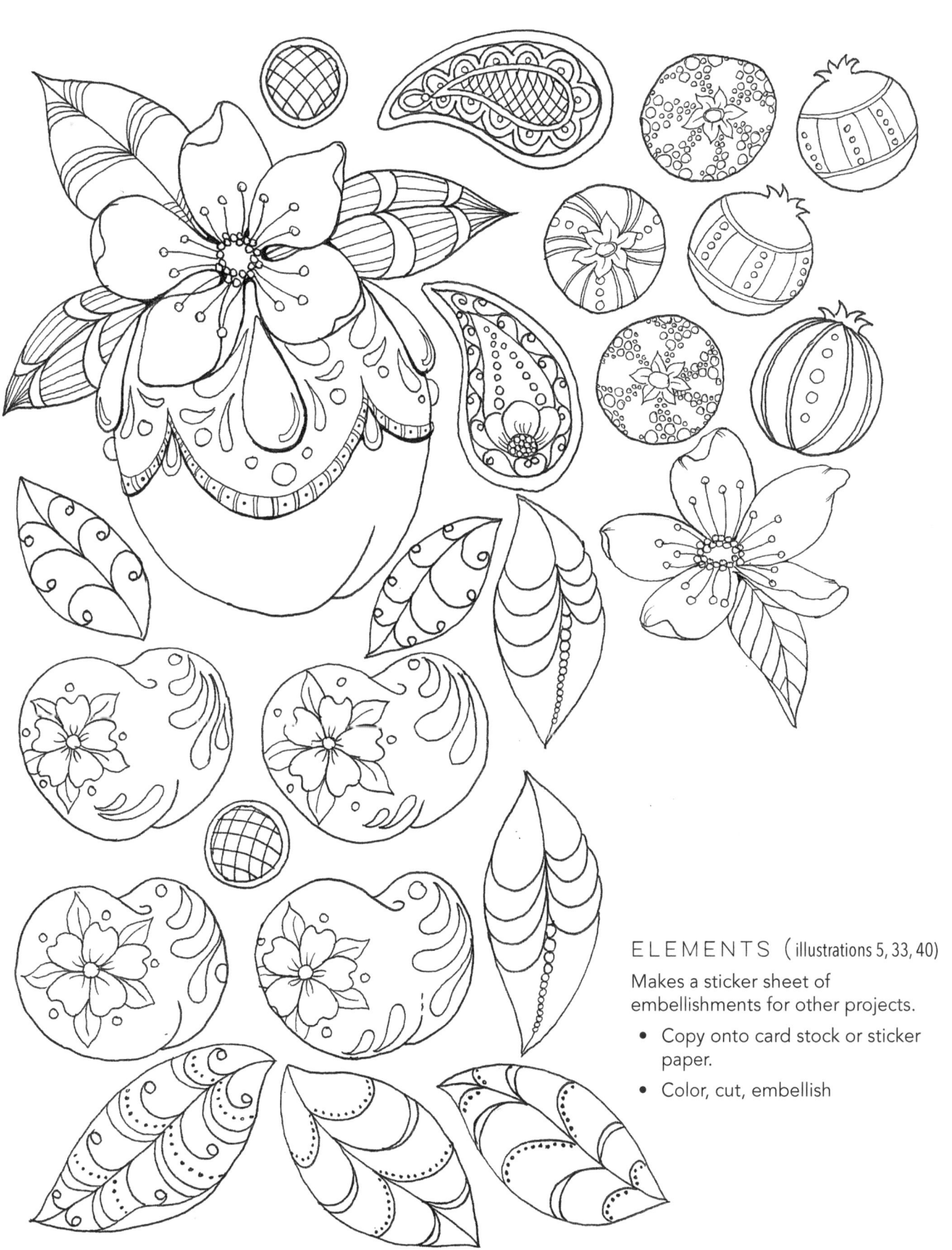

ELEMENTS (illustrations 5, 33, 40)

Makes a sticker sheet of embellishments for other projects.

- Copy onto card stock or sticker paper.
- Color, cut, embellish

ILLUSTRATION 6

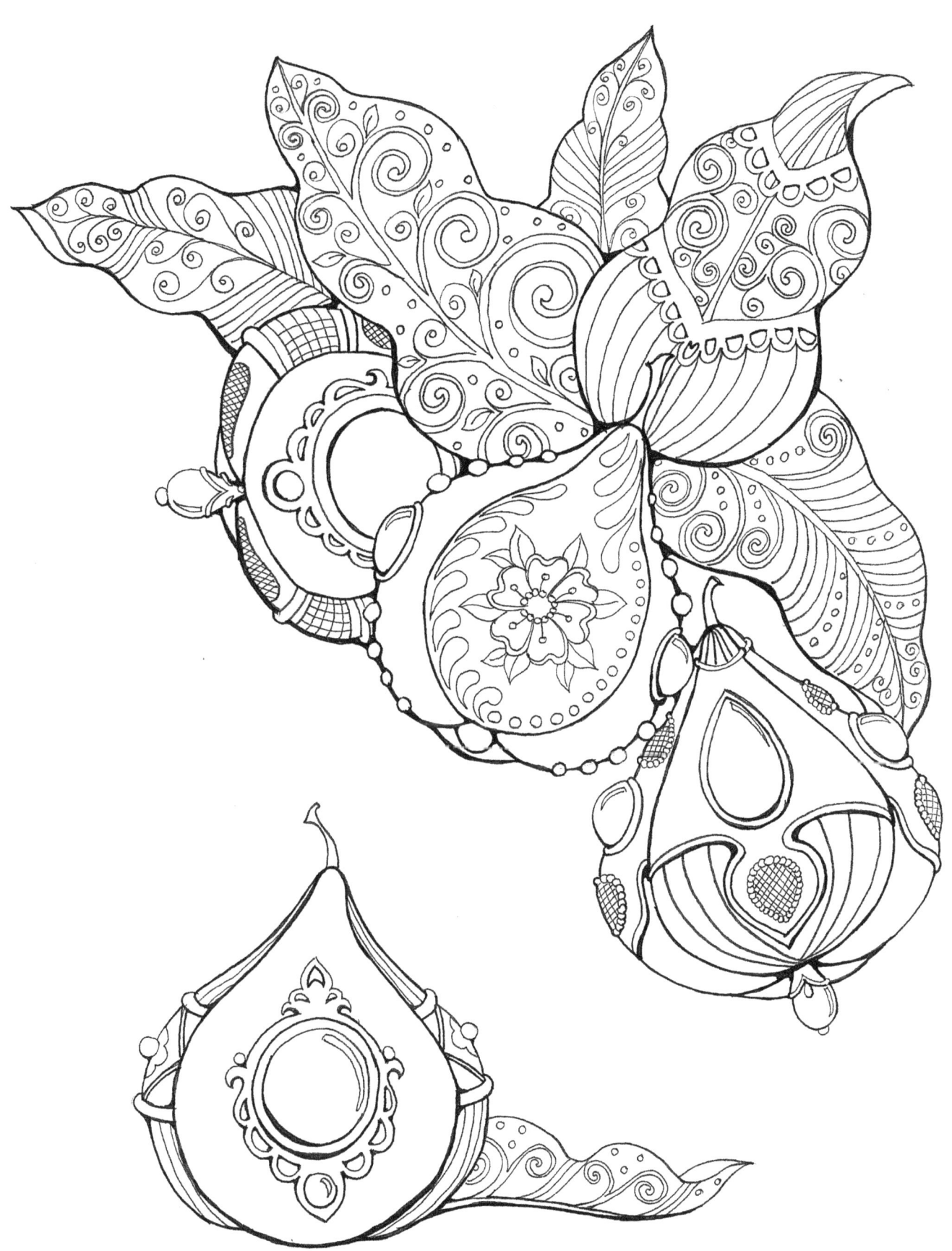

ILLUSTRATION 7

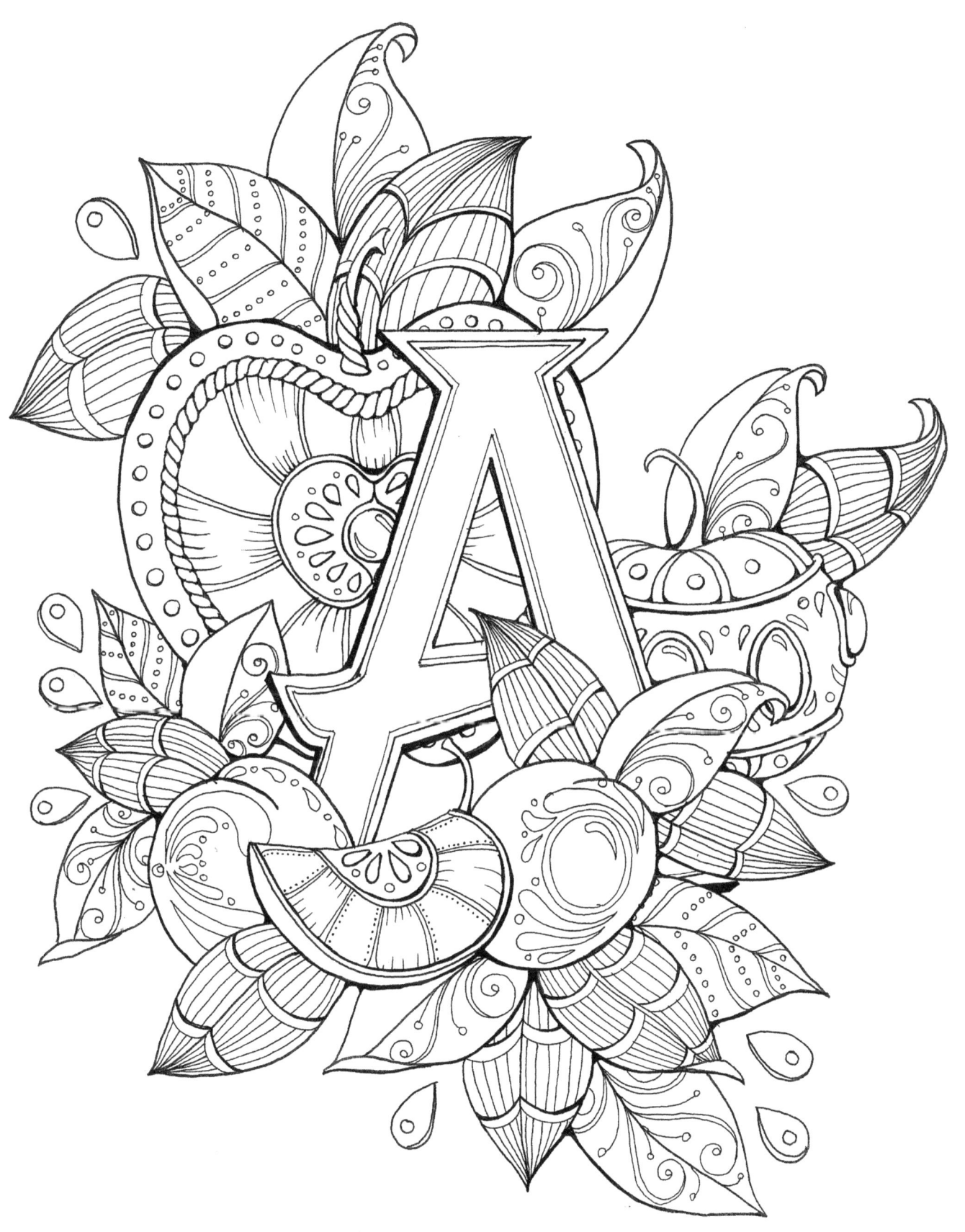

ILLUSTRATION 8

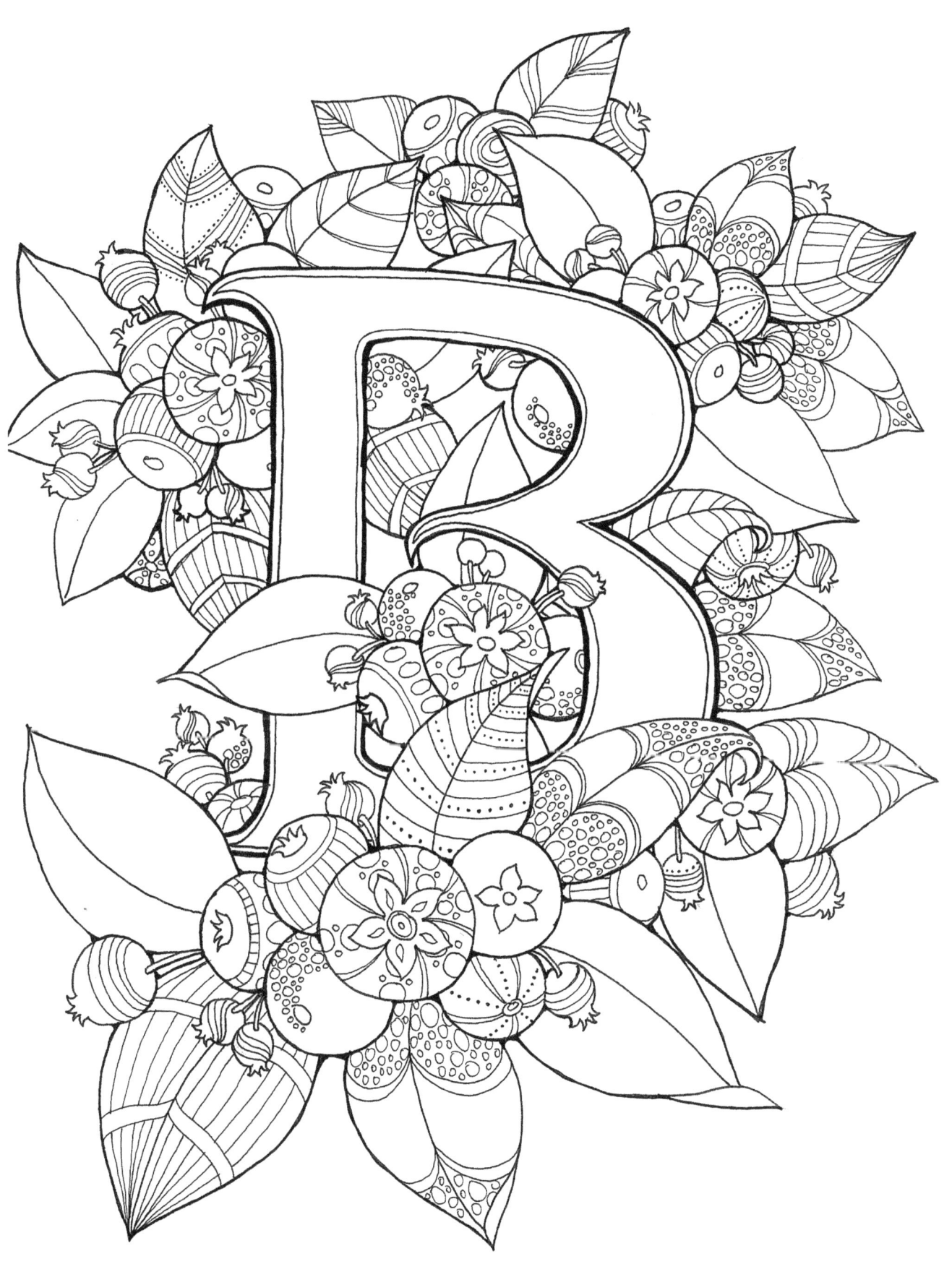

ILLUSTRATION 9

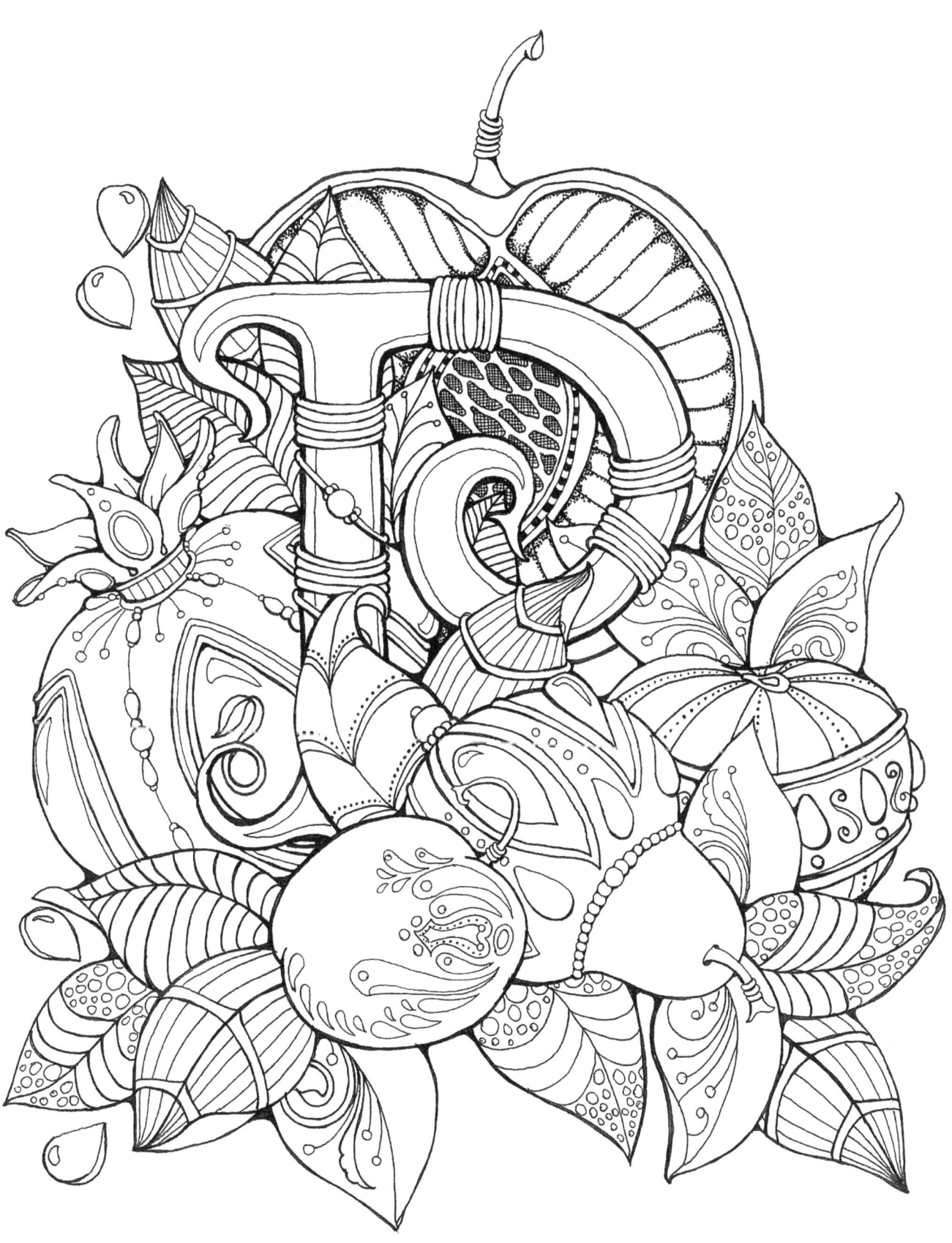

ILLUSTRATION 10

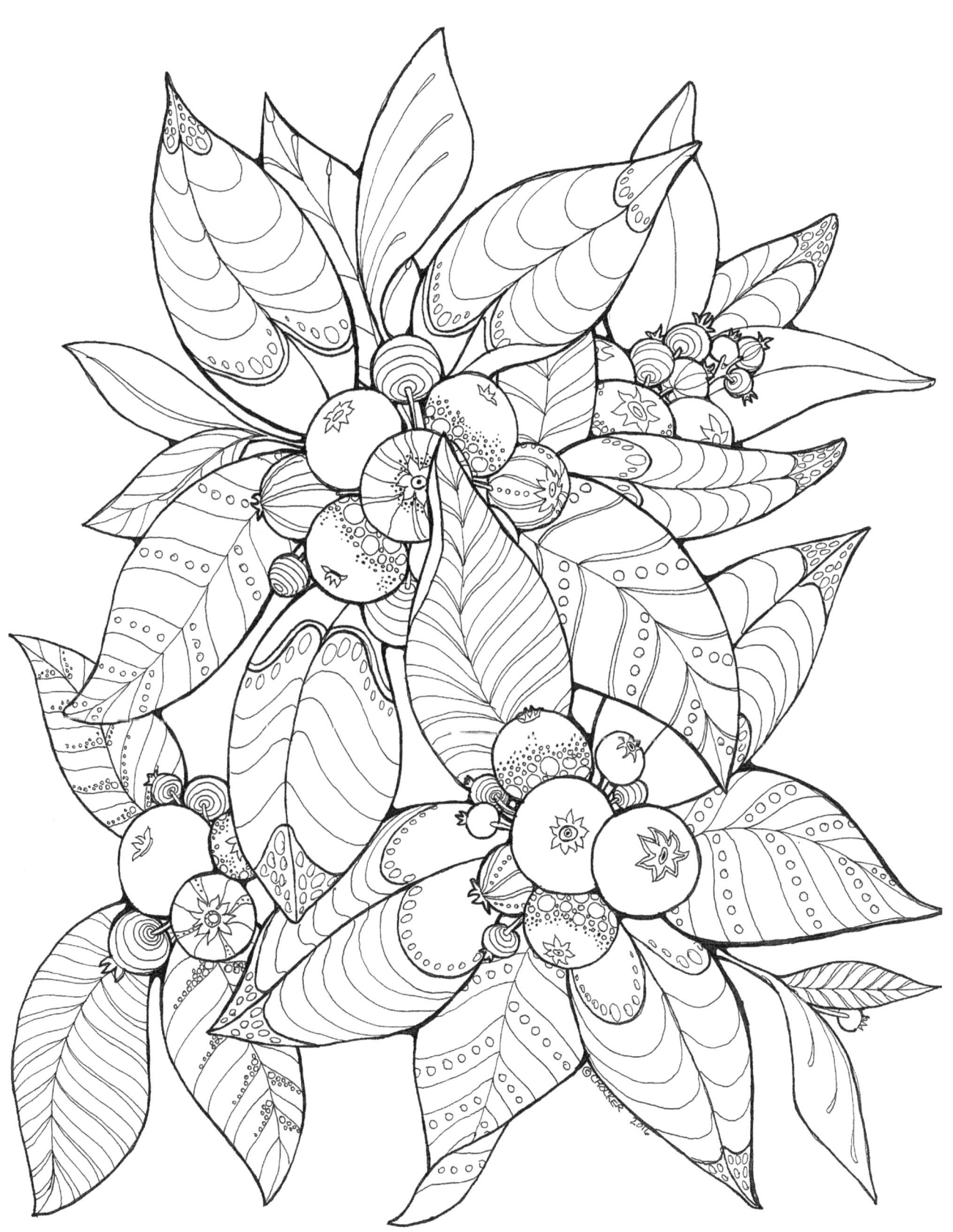

ILLUSTRATION 11

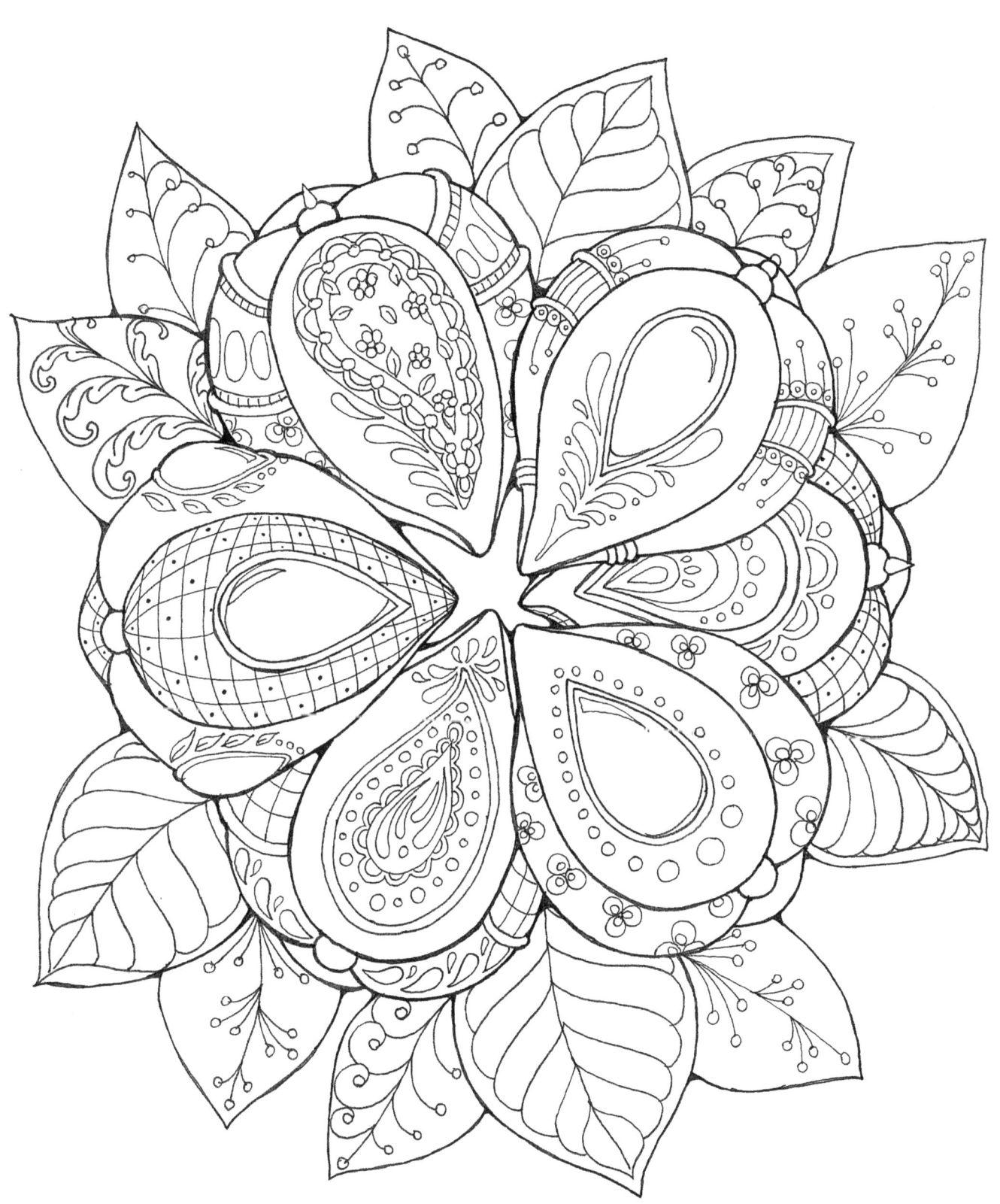

ILLUSTRATION 12

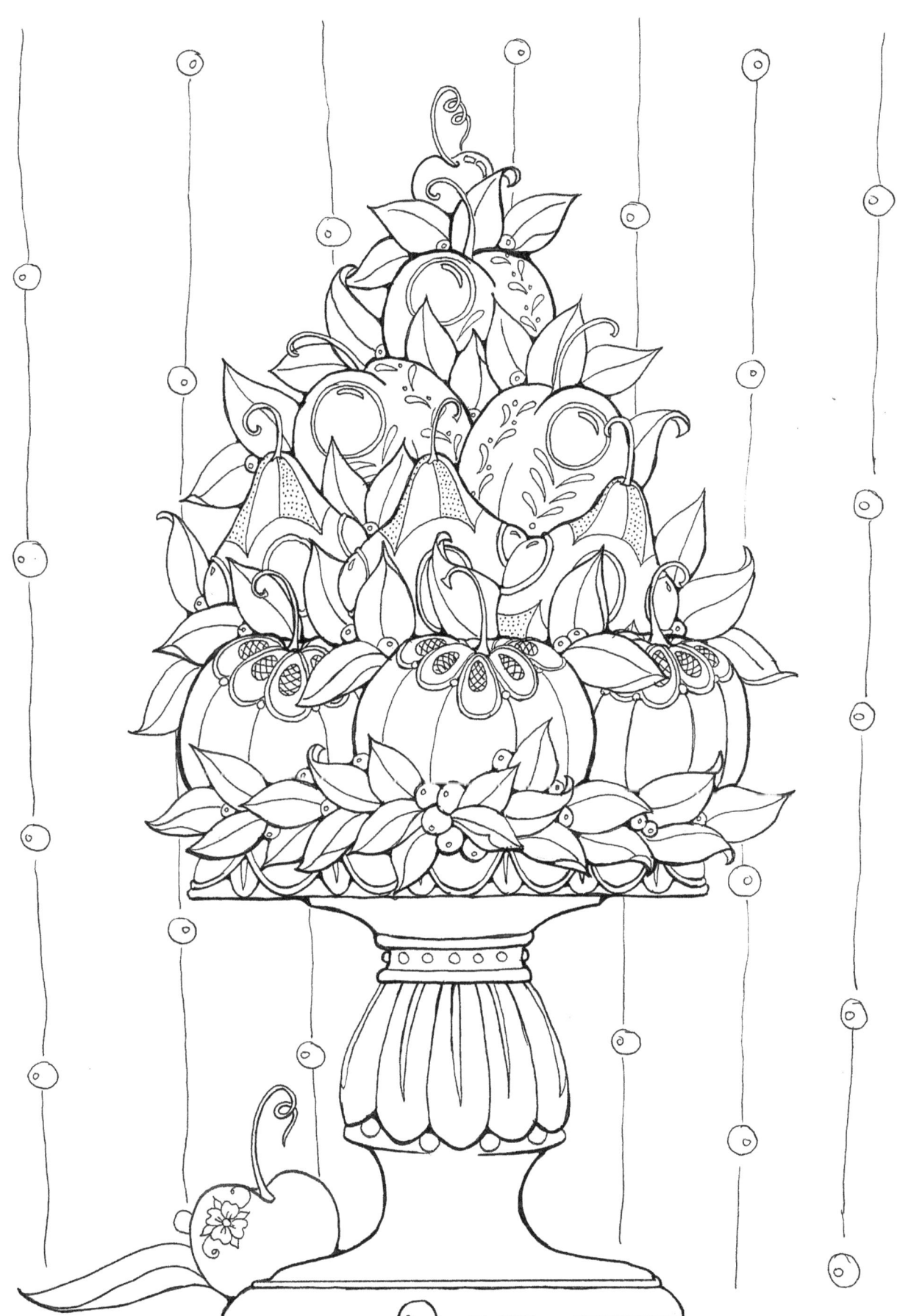

ILLUSTRATION 13

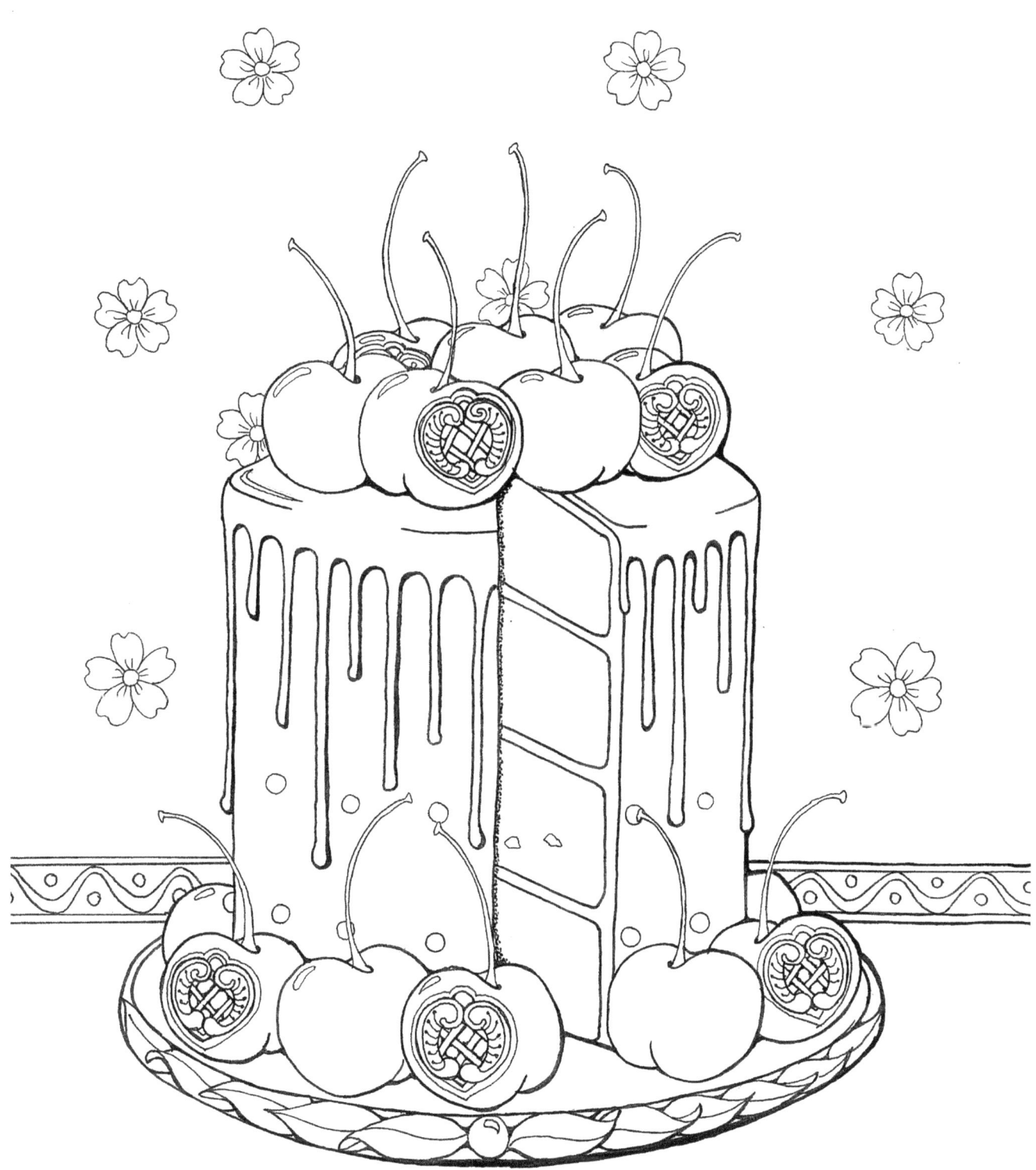

ILLUSTRATION 14

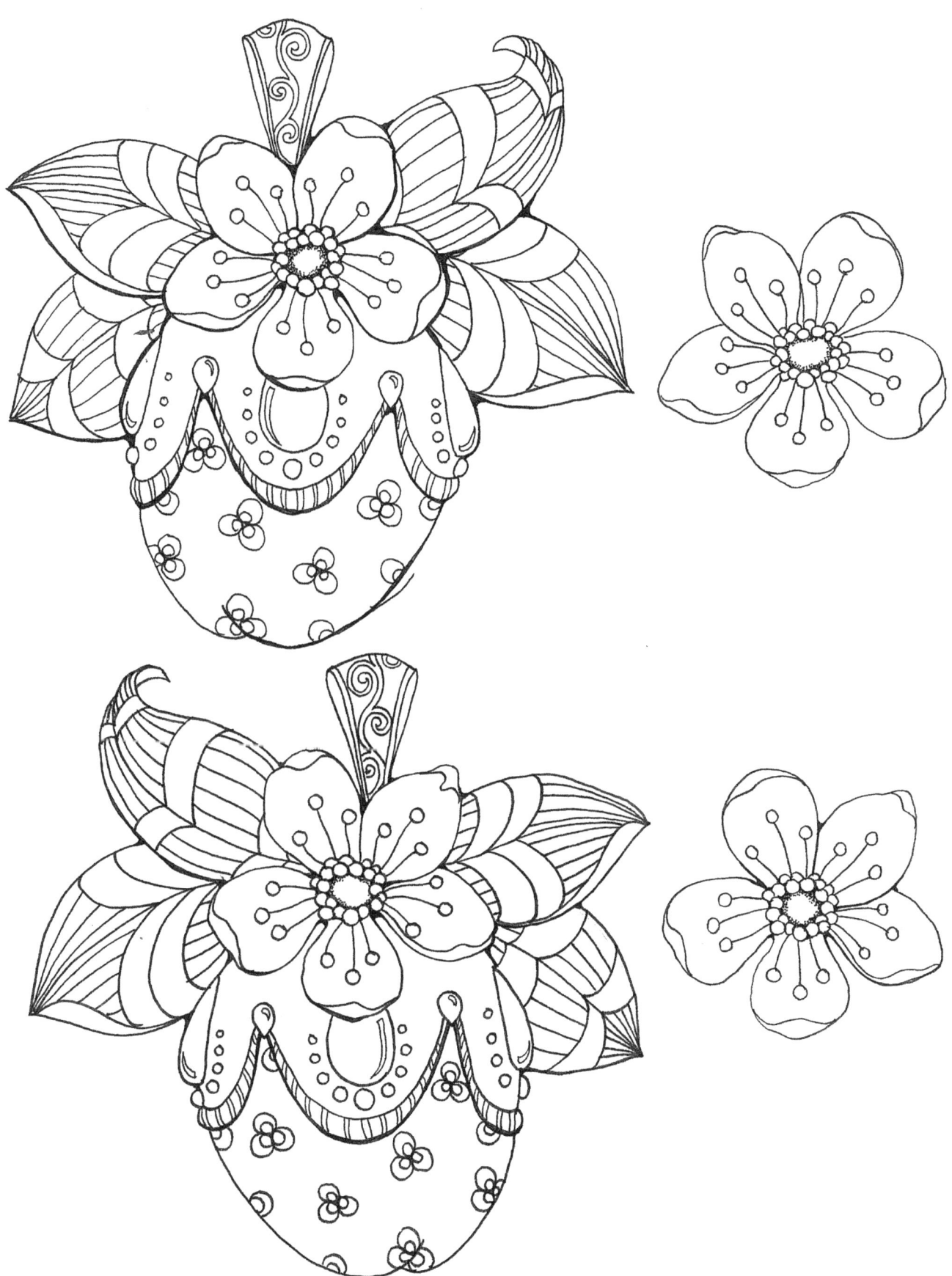

ILLUSTRATION 15

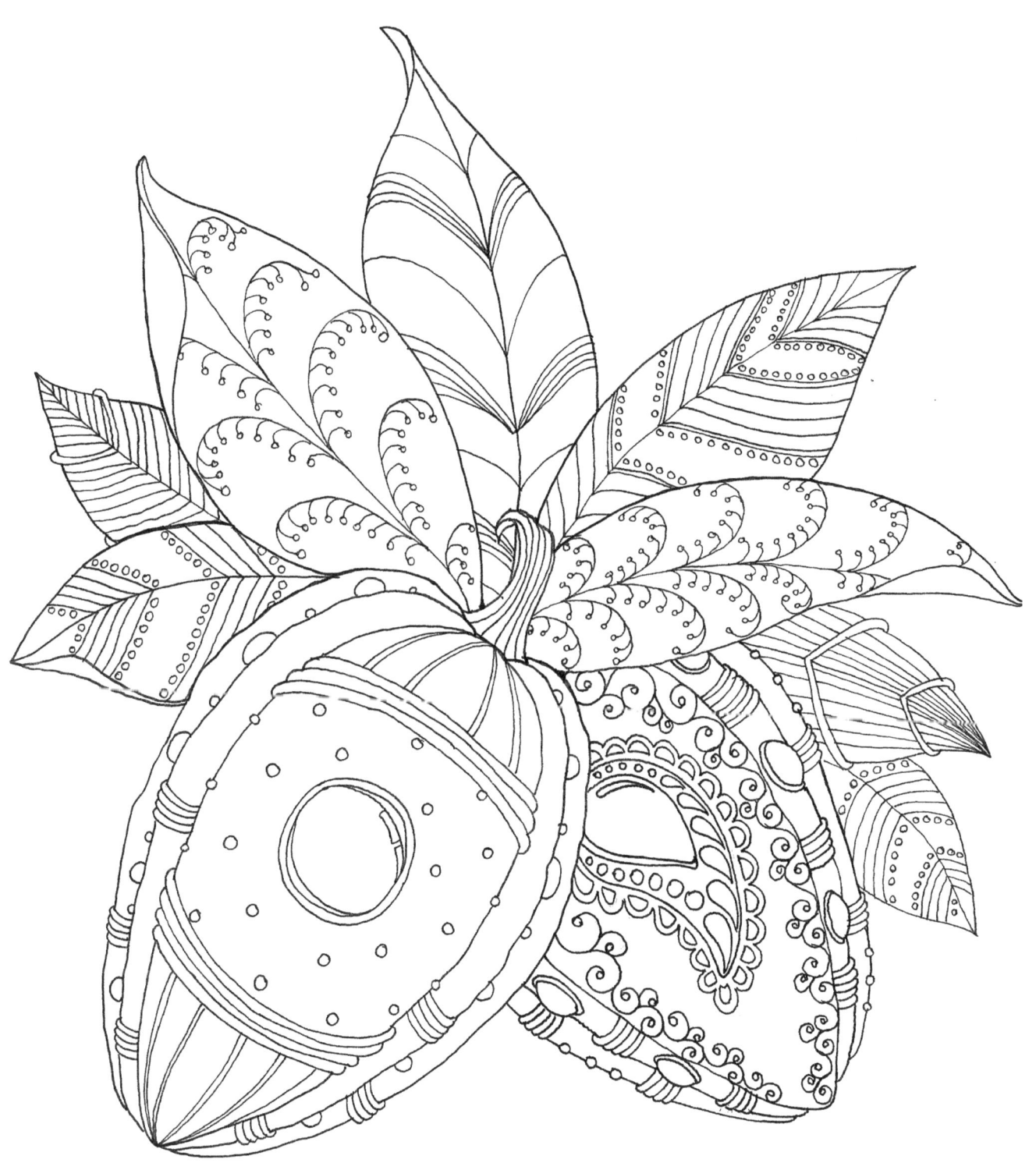

ILLUSTRATION 16

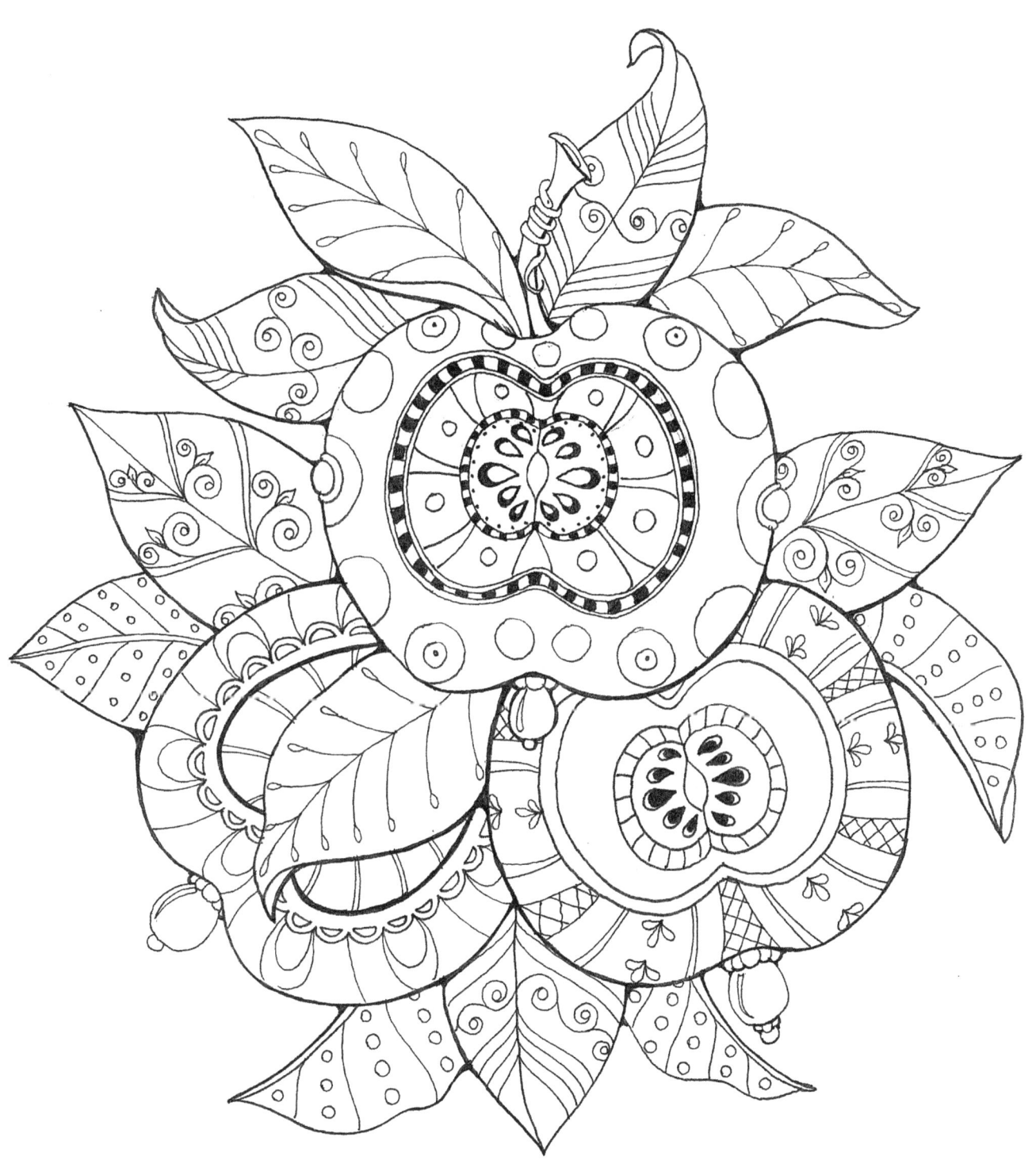

ILLUSTRATION 17

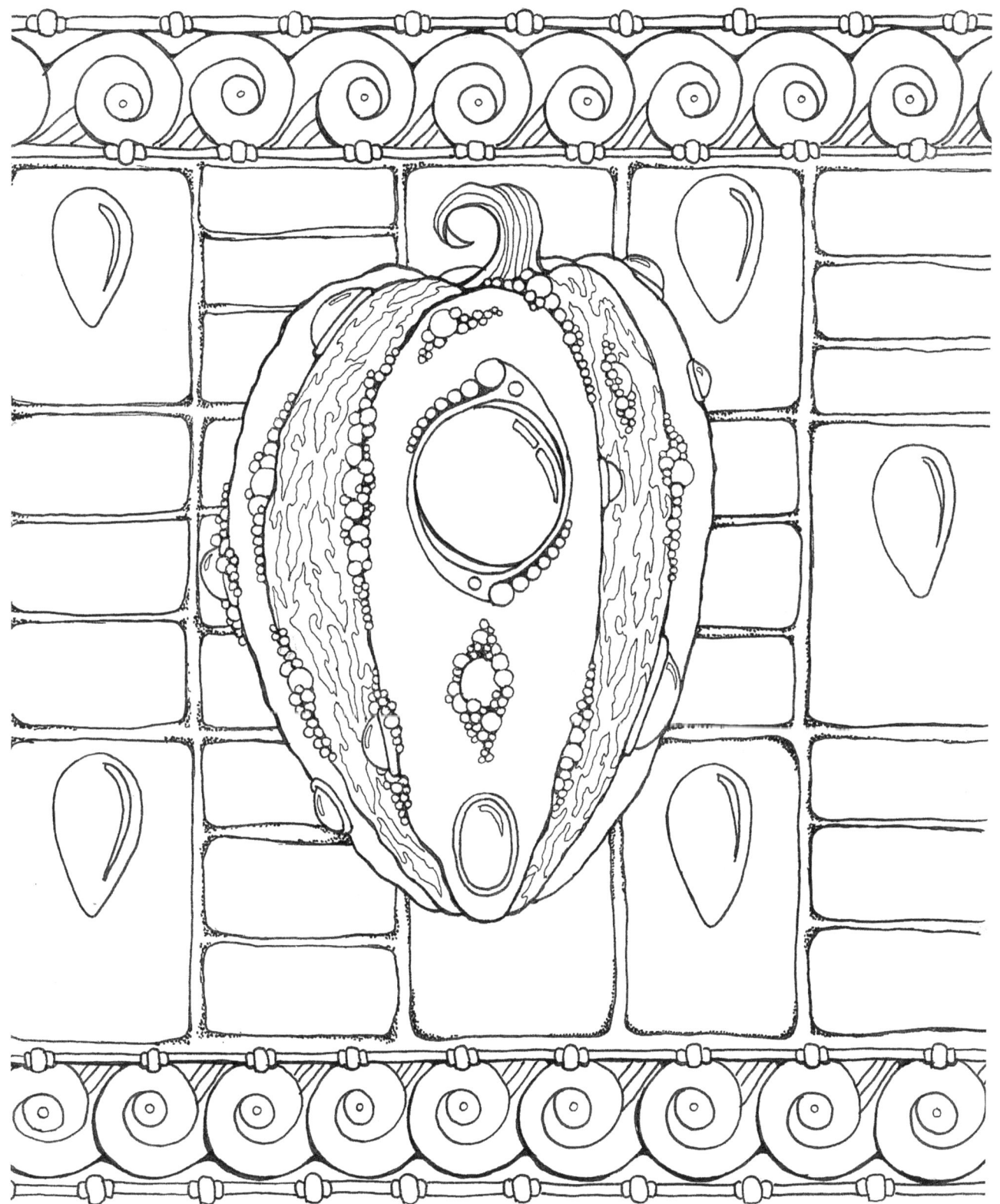

ILLUSTRATION 18

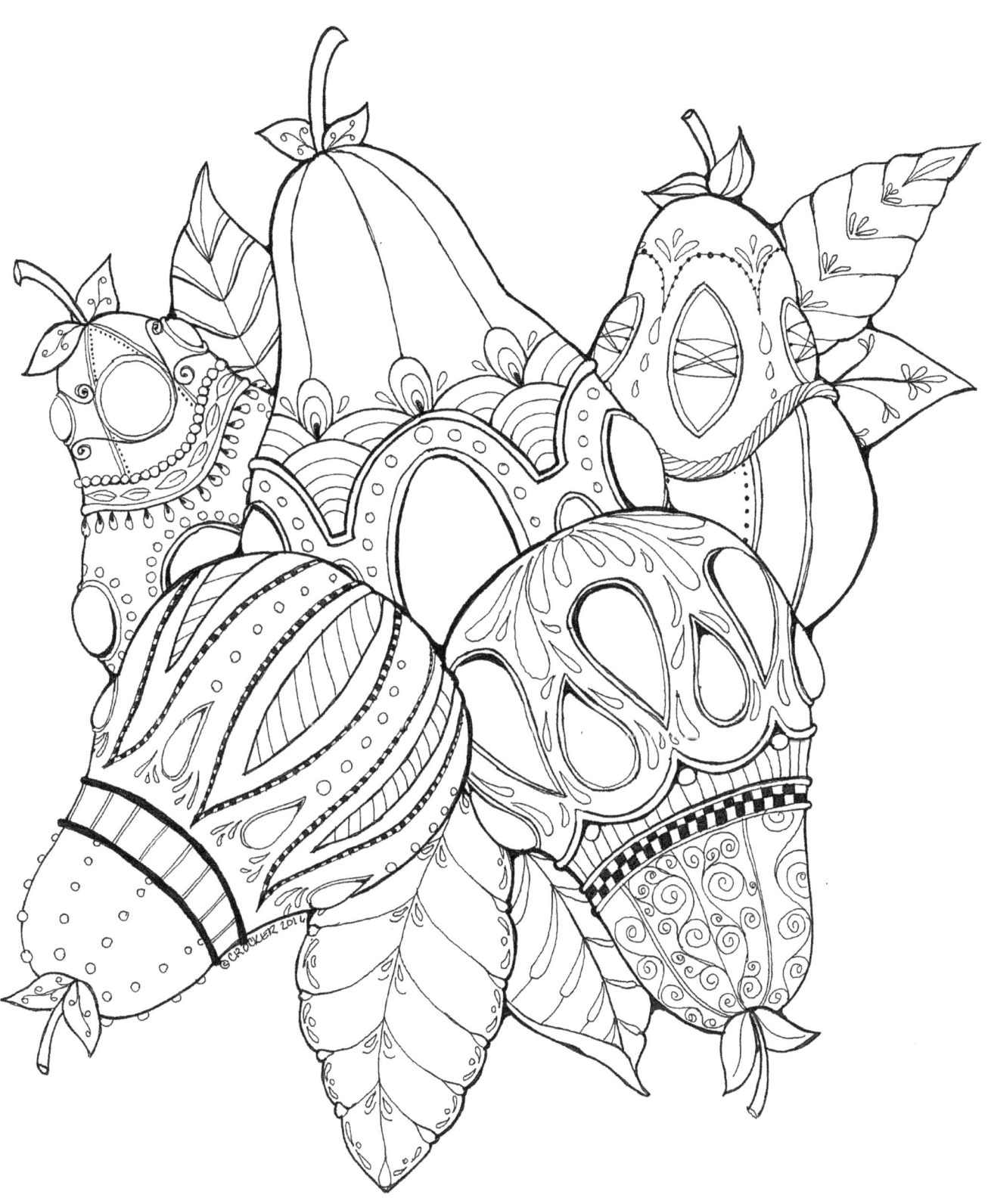

ILLUSTRATION 19

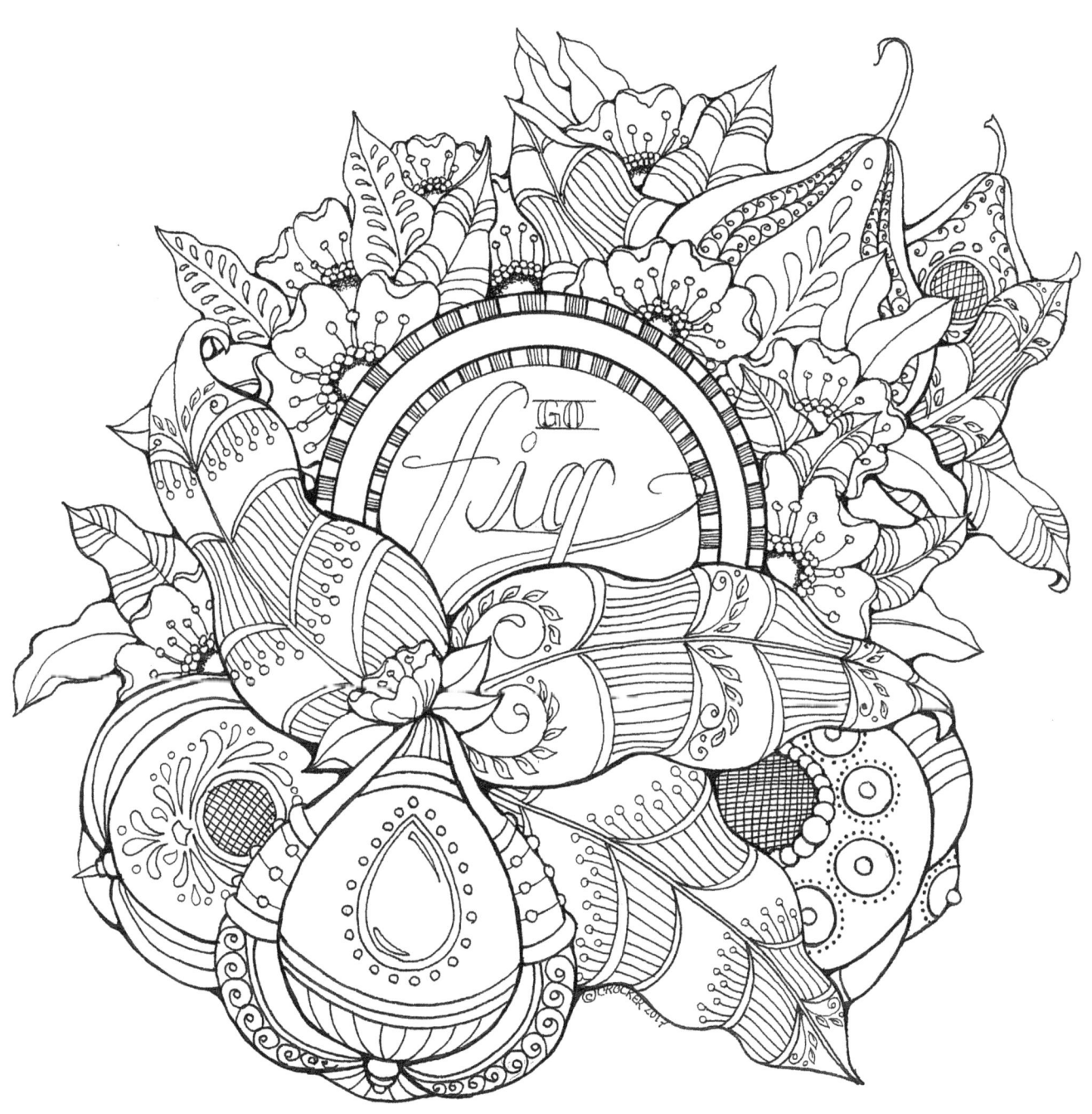

ILLUSTRATION 20

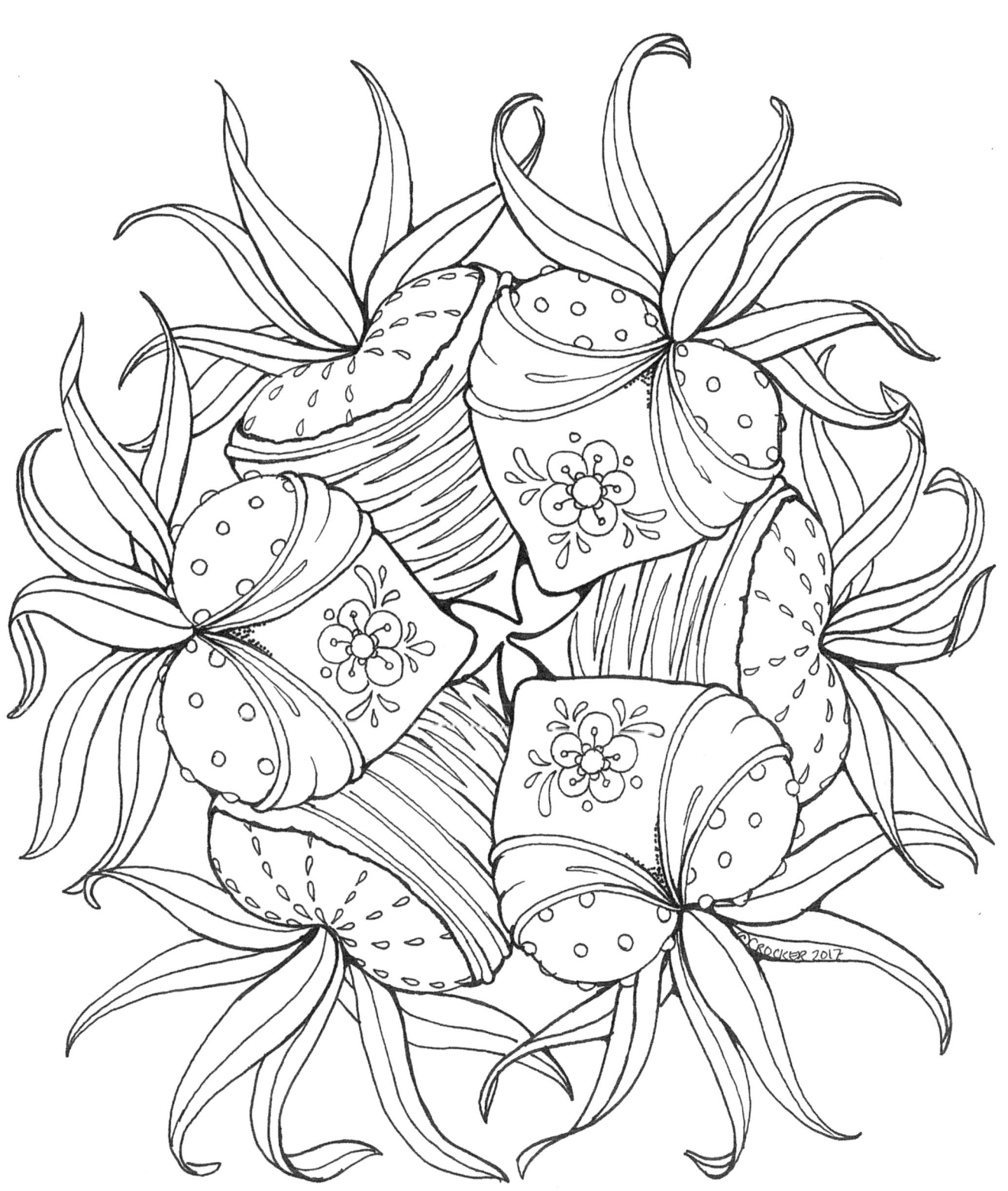

ILLUSTRATION 21

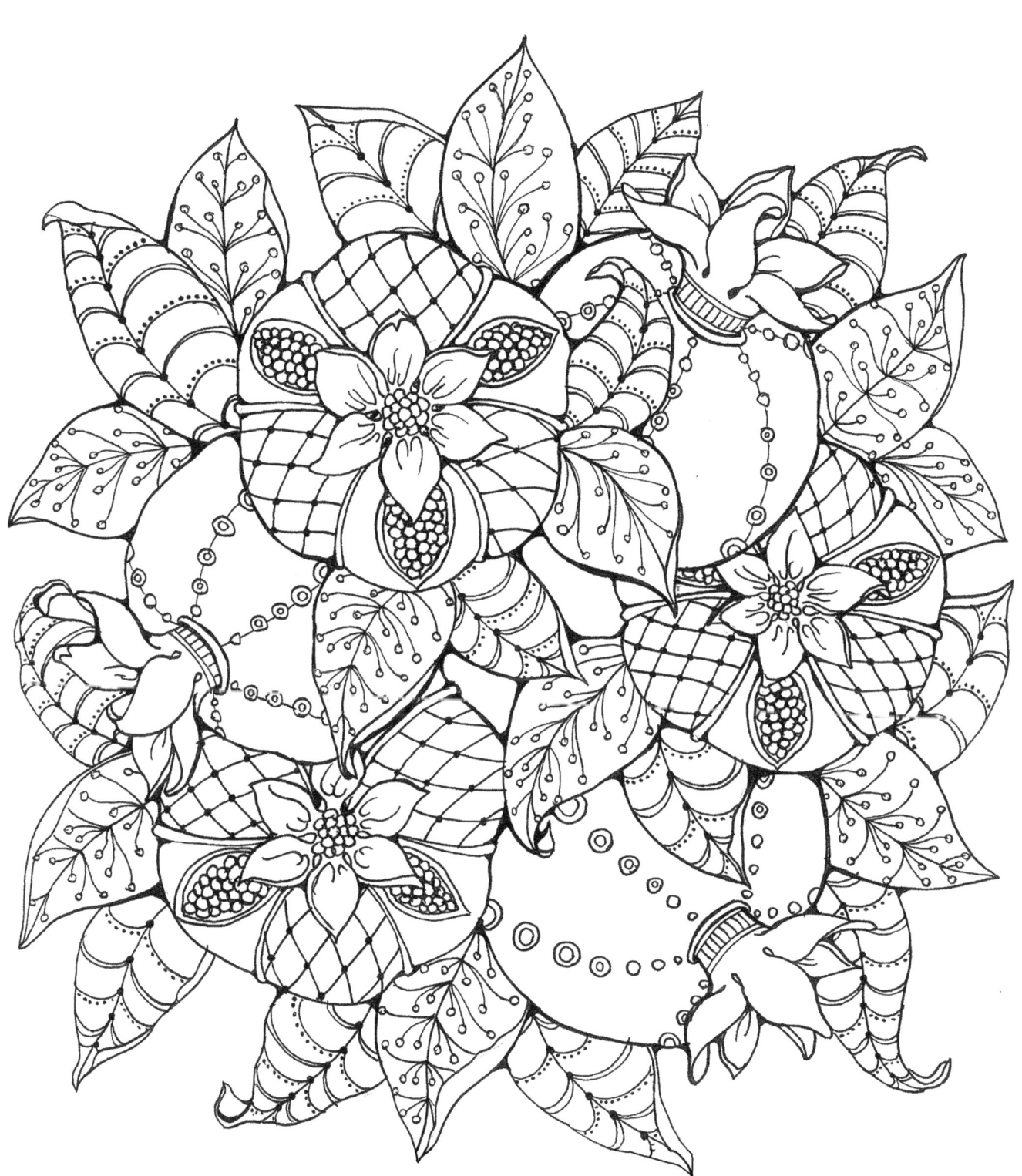

ILLUSTRATION 22

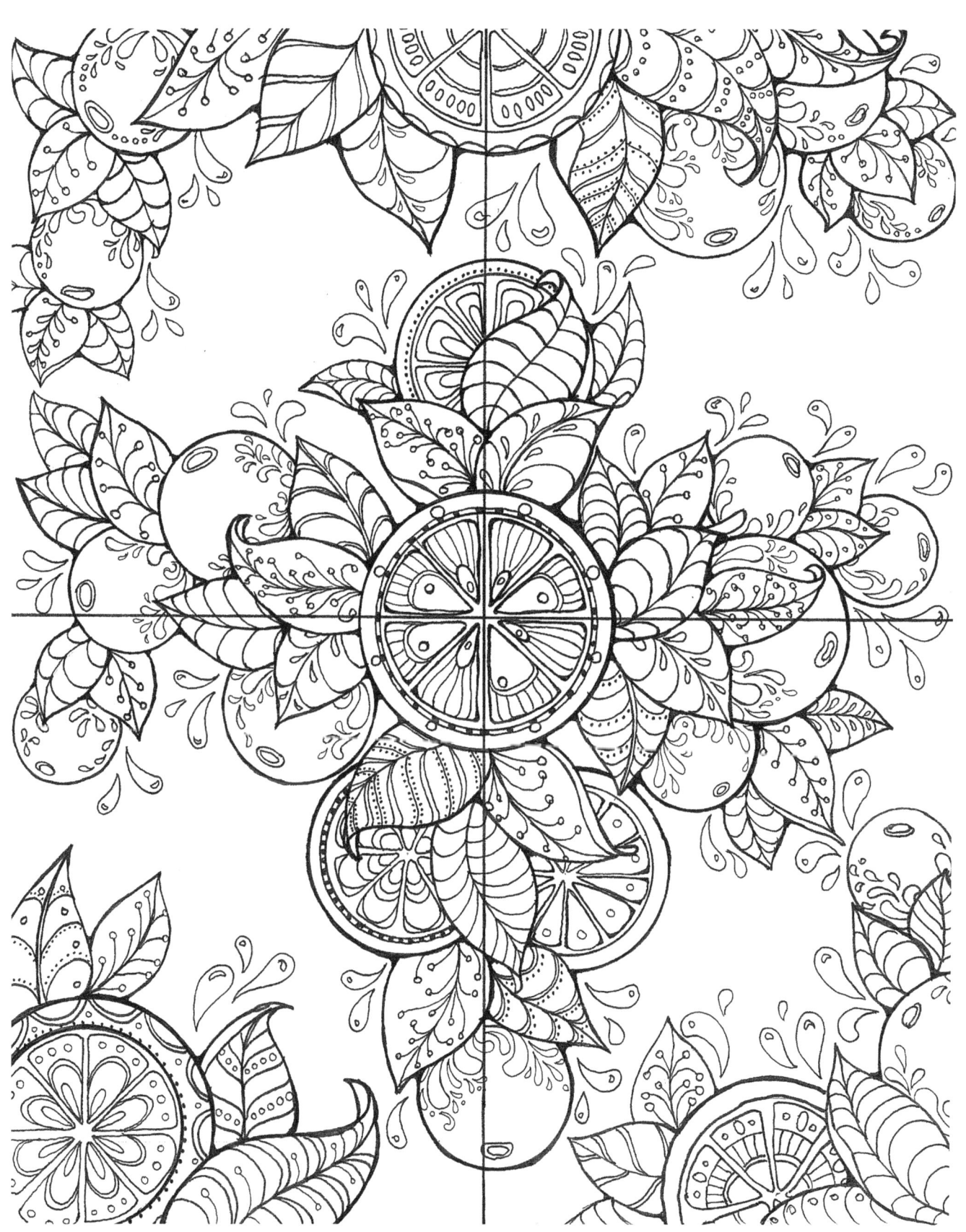

ILLUSTRATION 23

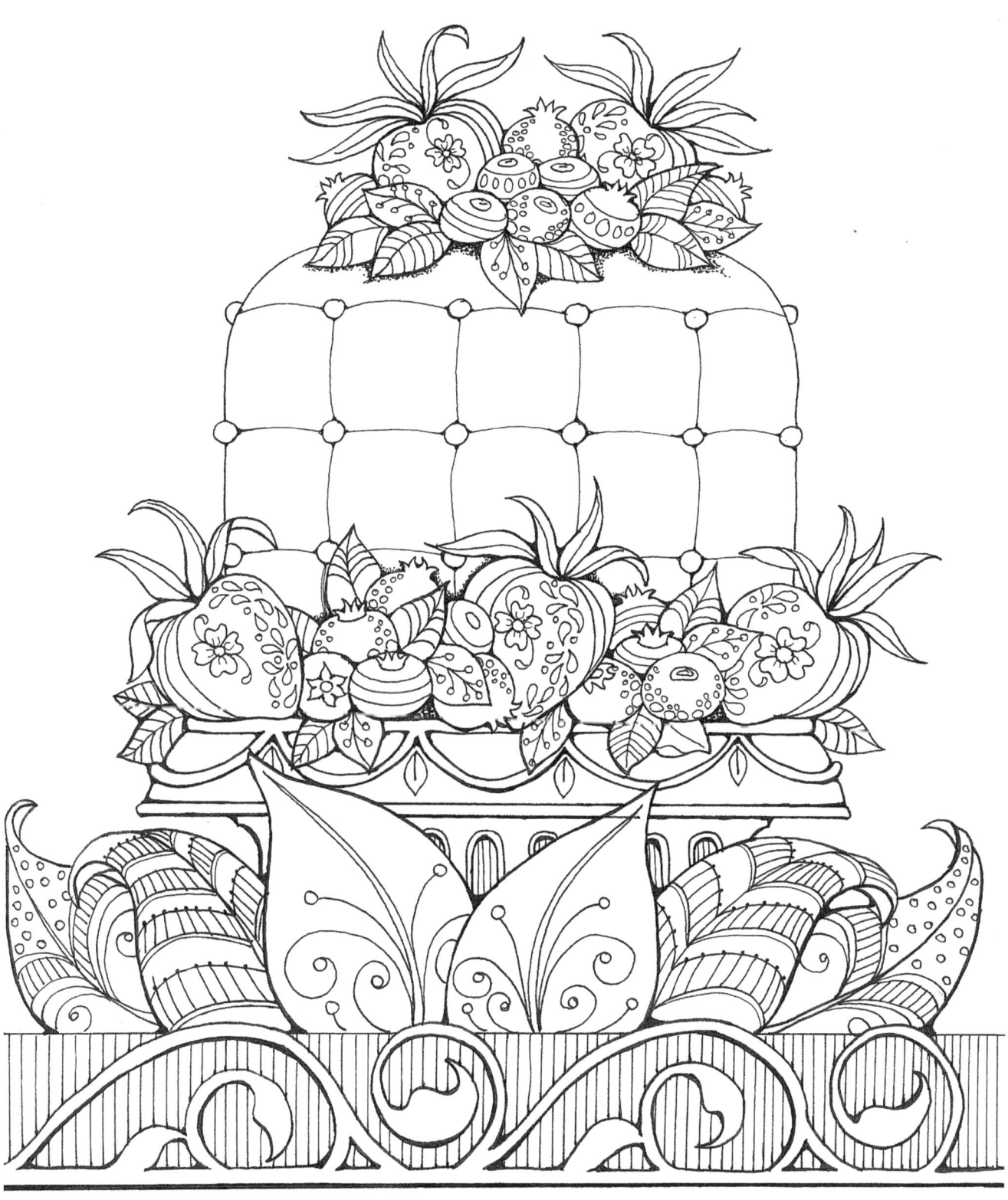

ILLUSTRATION 24

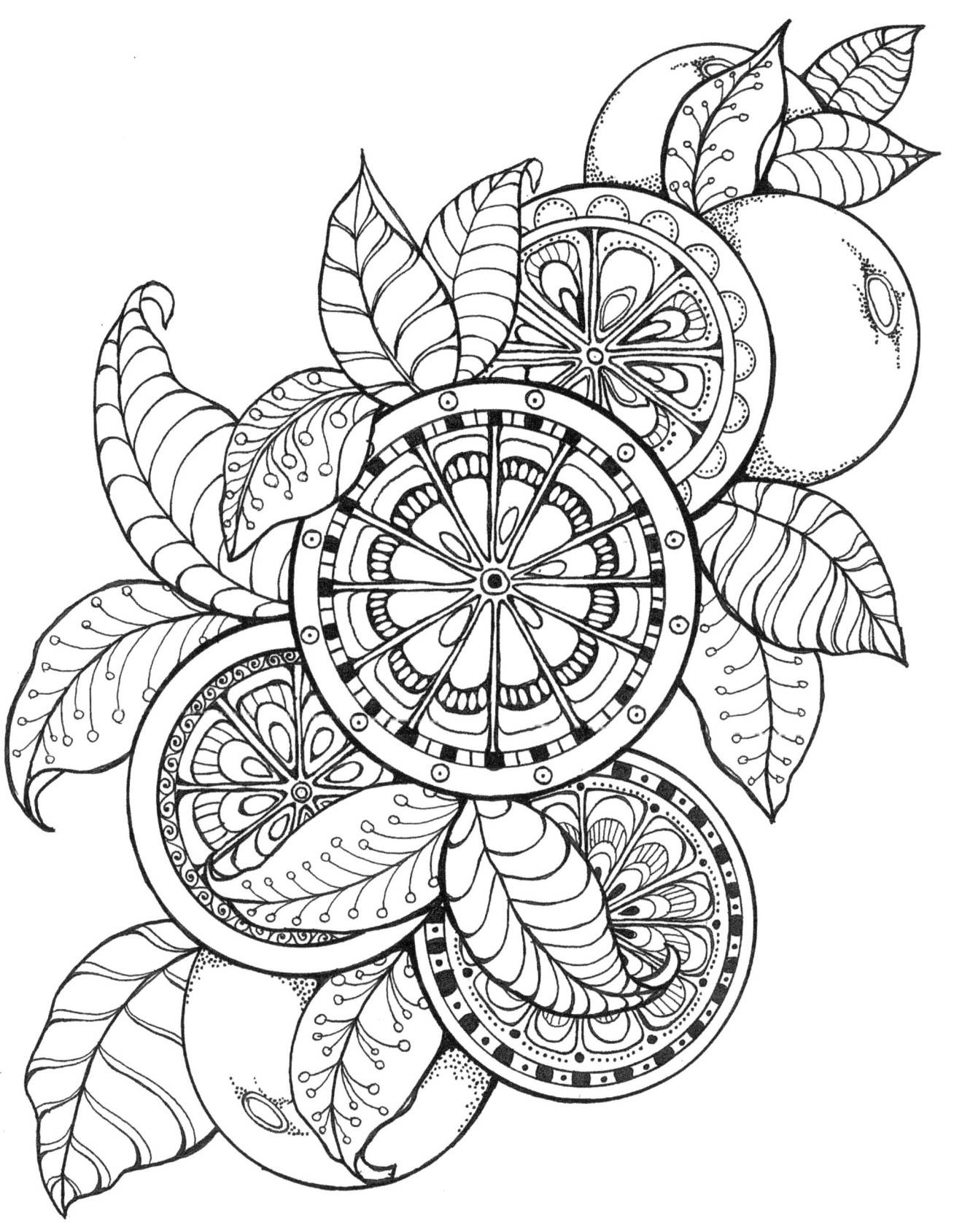

ILLUSTRATION 25

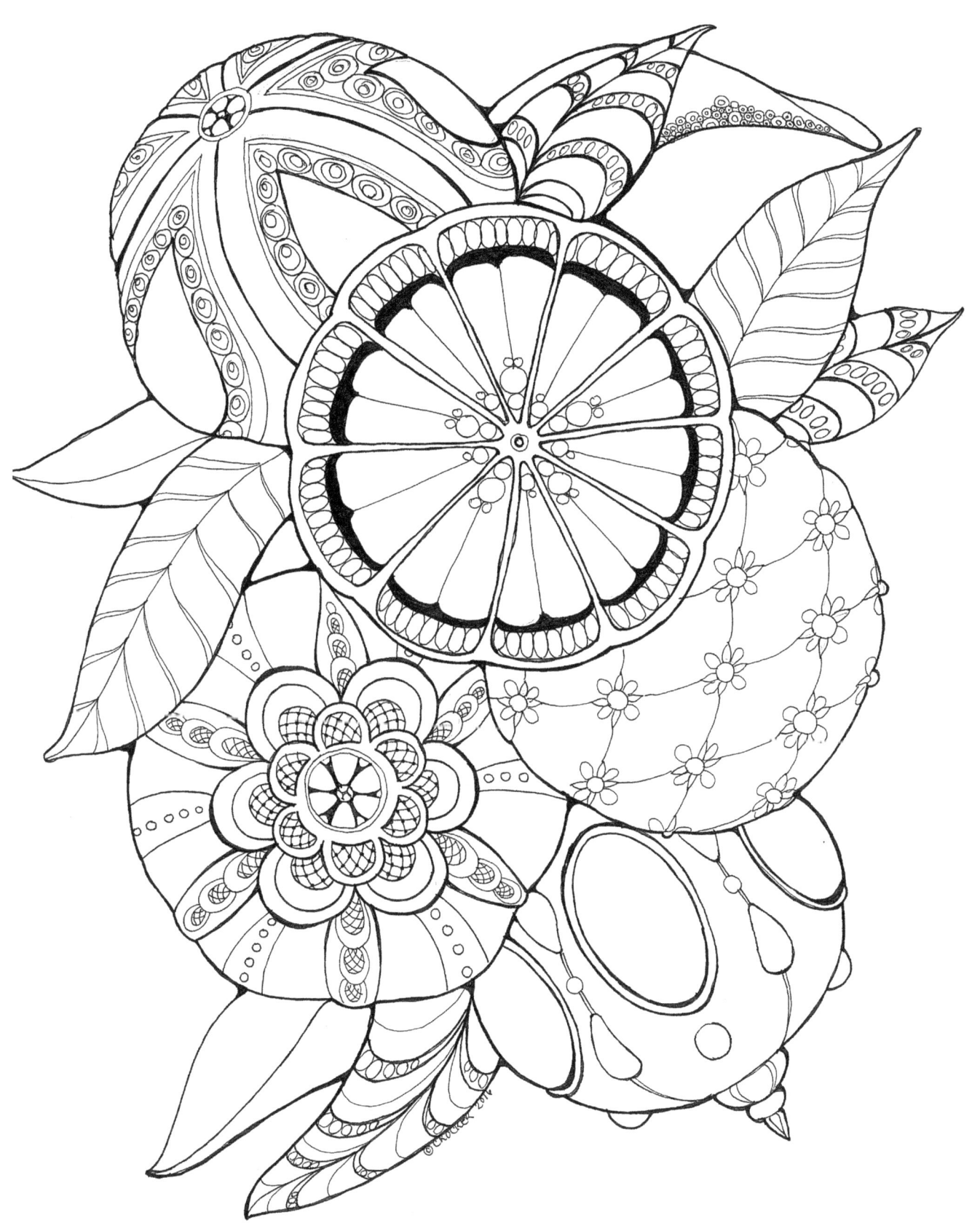

ILLUSTRATION 26

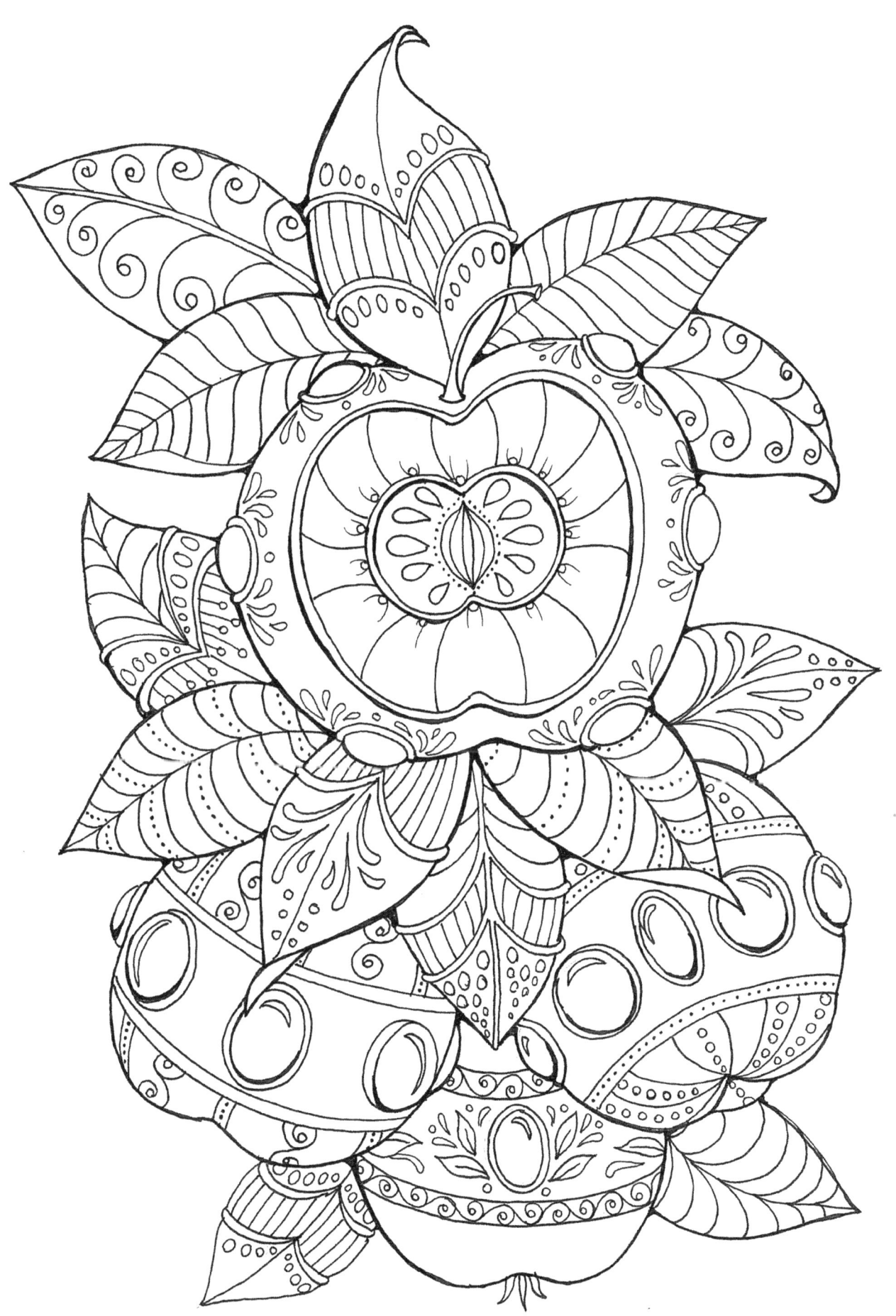

ILLUSTRATION 27

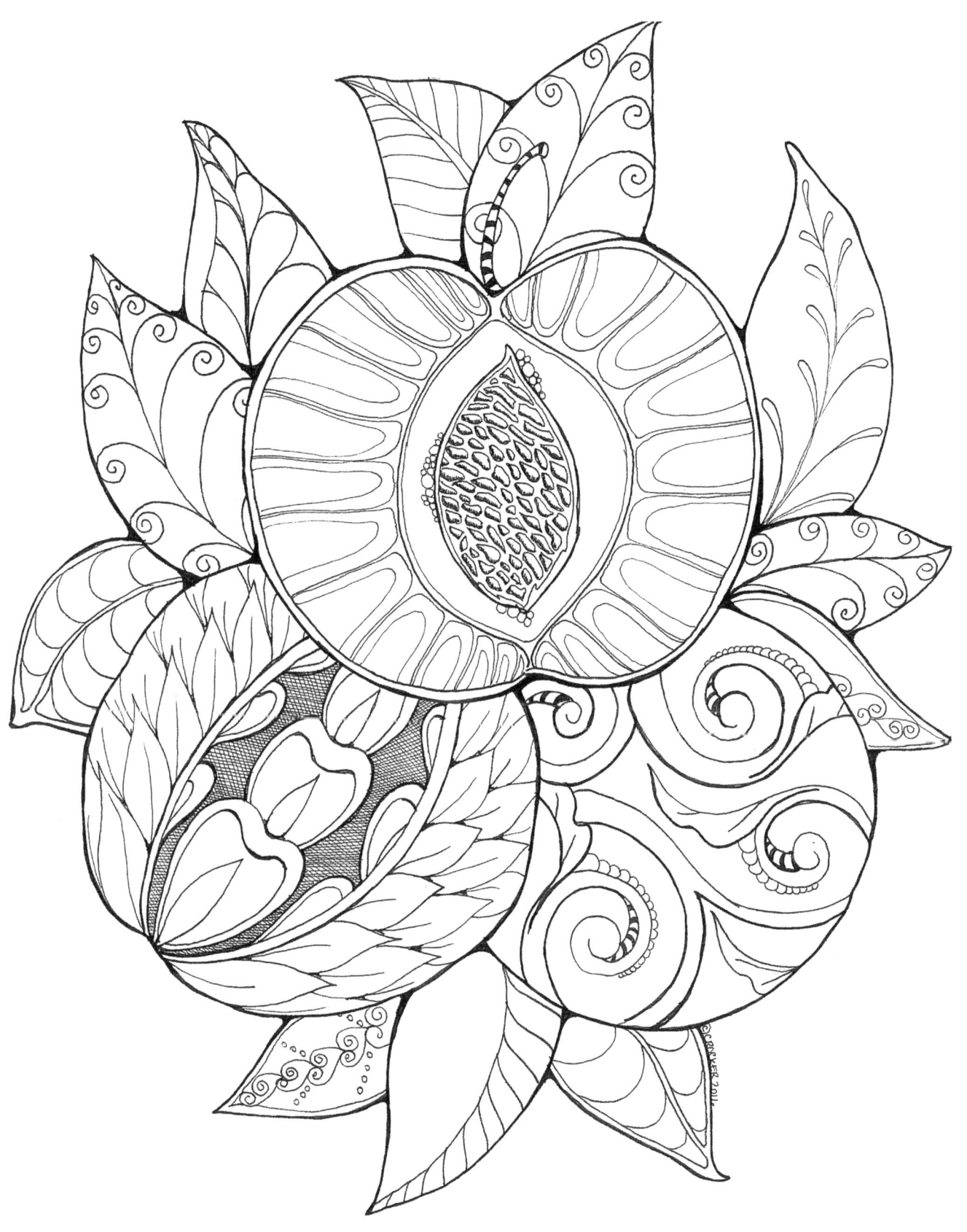

ILLUSTRATION 28

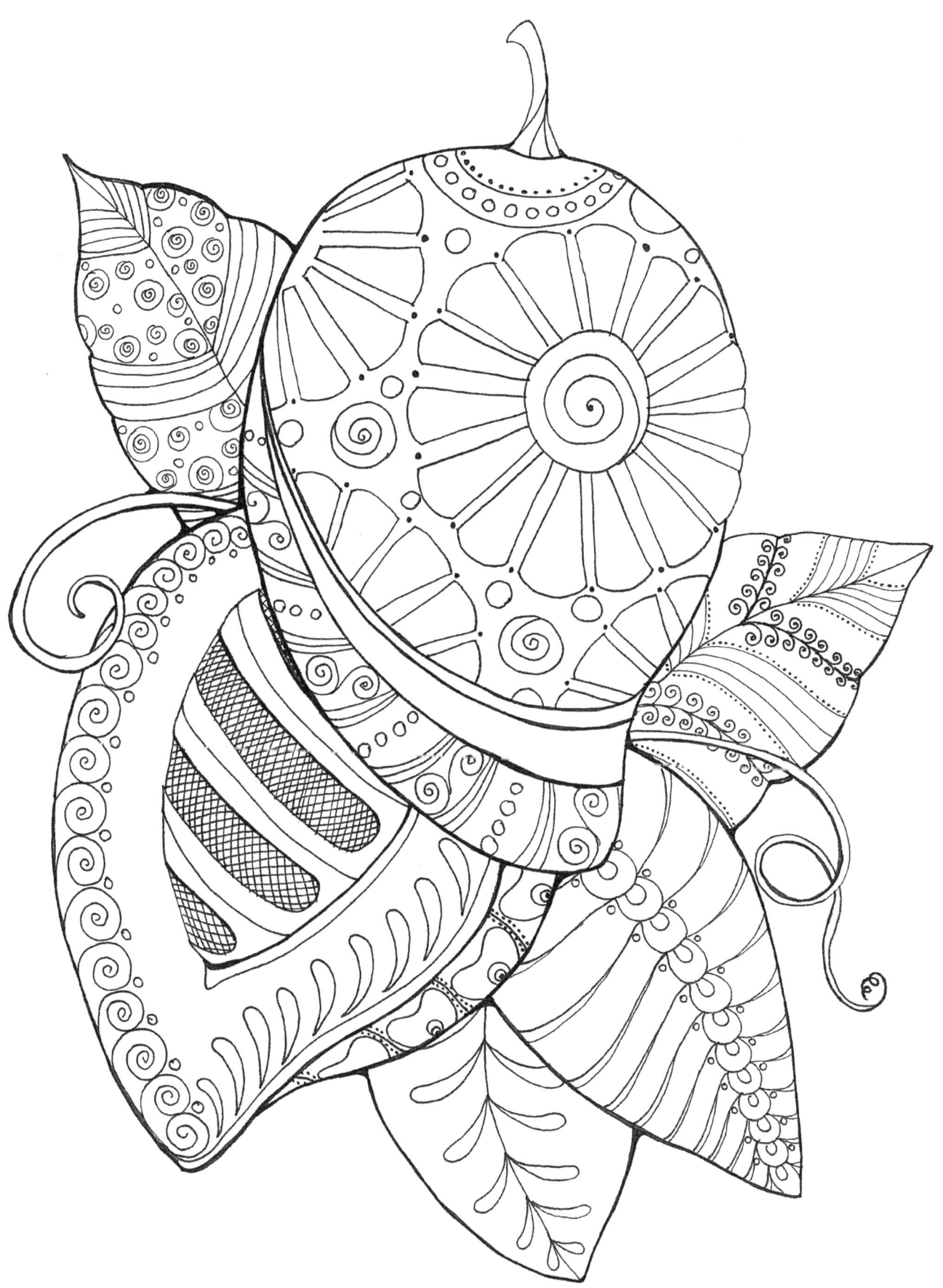

ILLUSTRATION 29

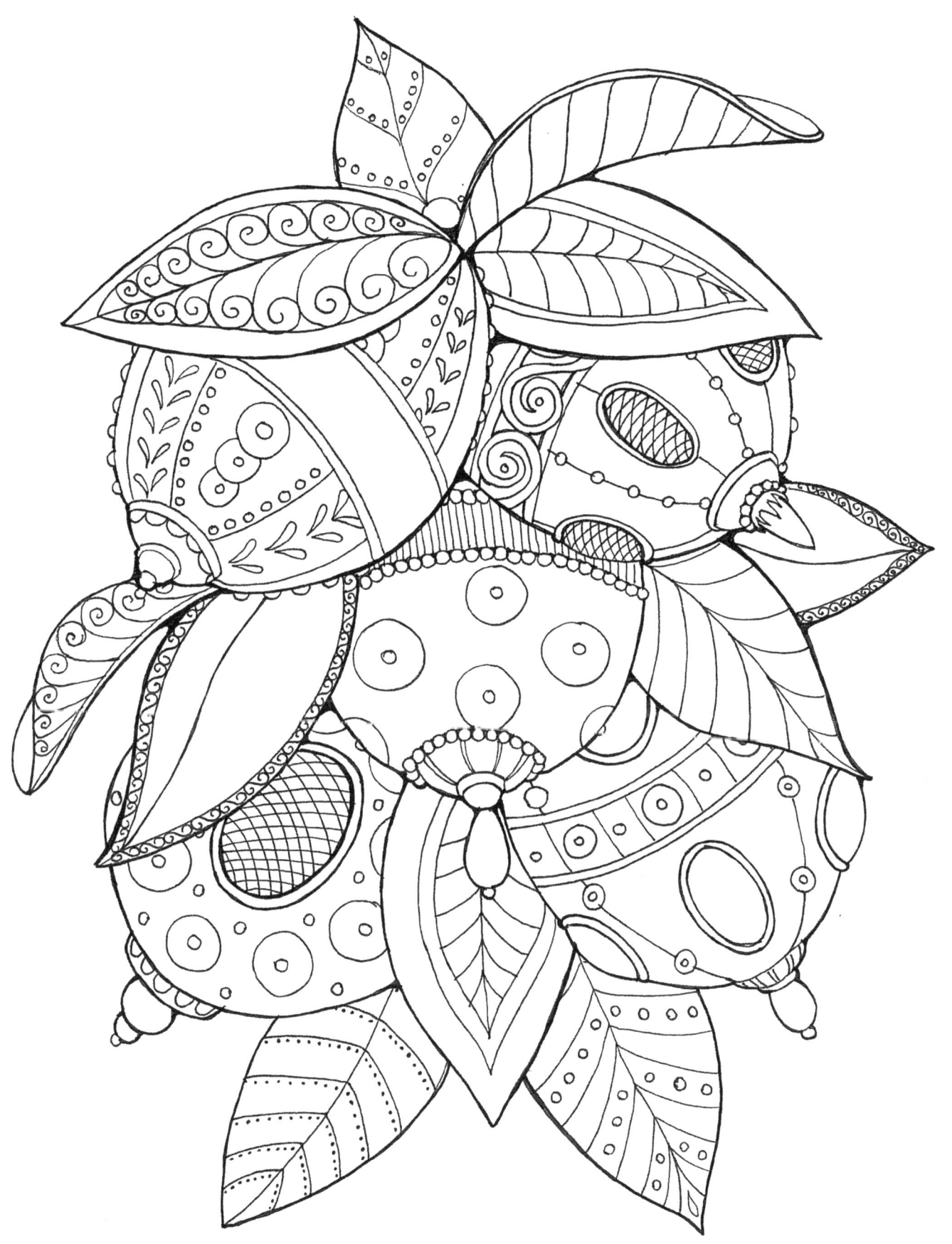

ILLUSTRATION 30

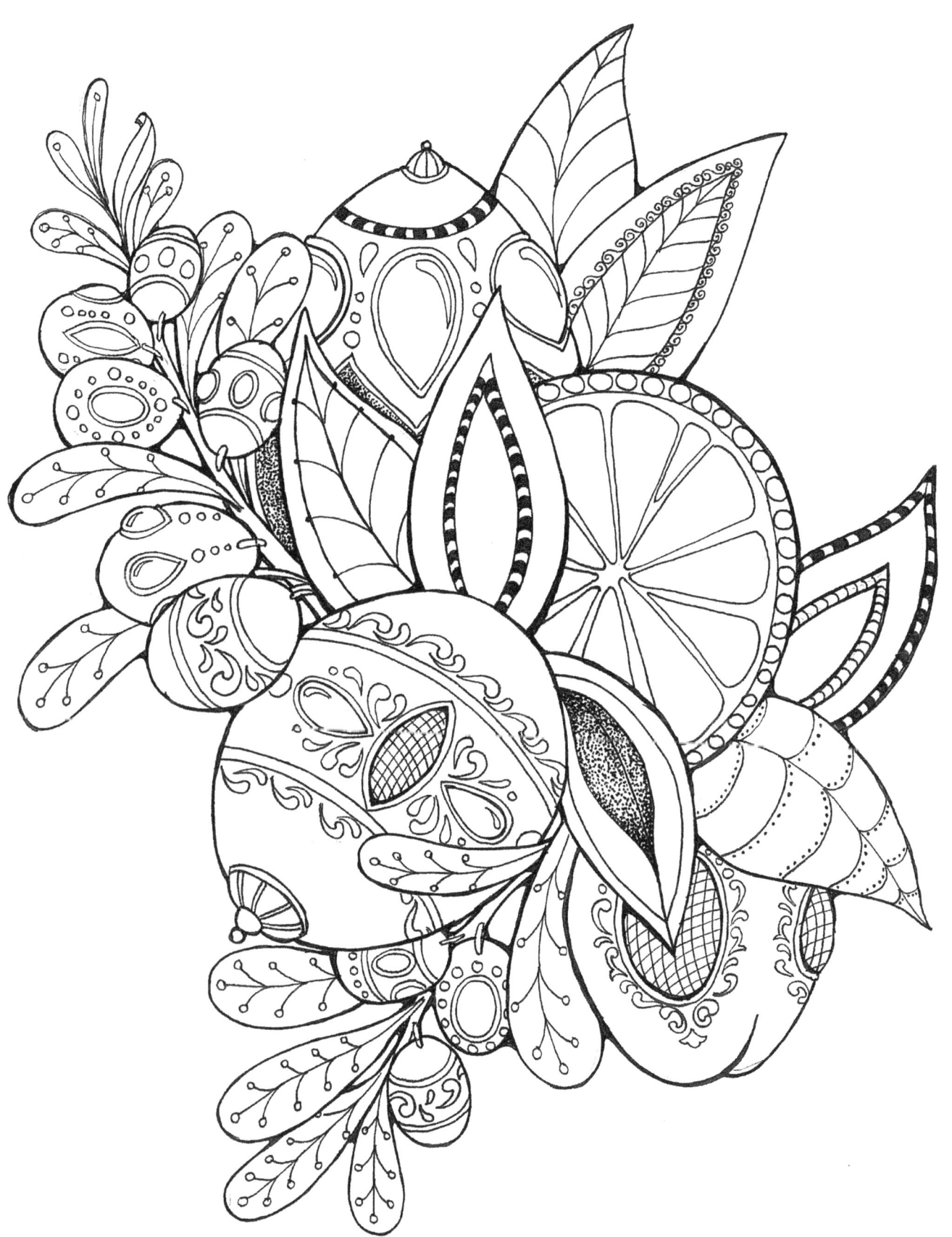

ILLUSTRATION 31

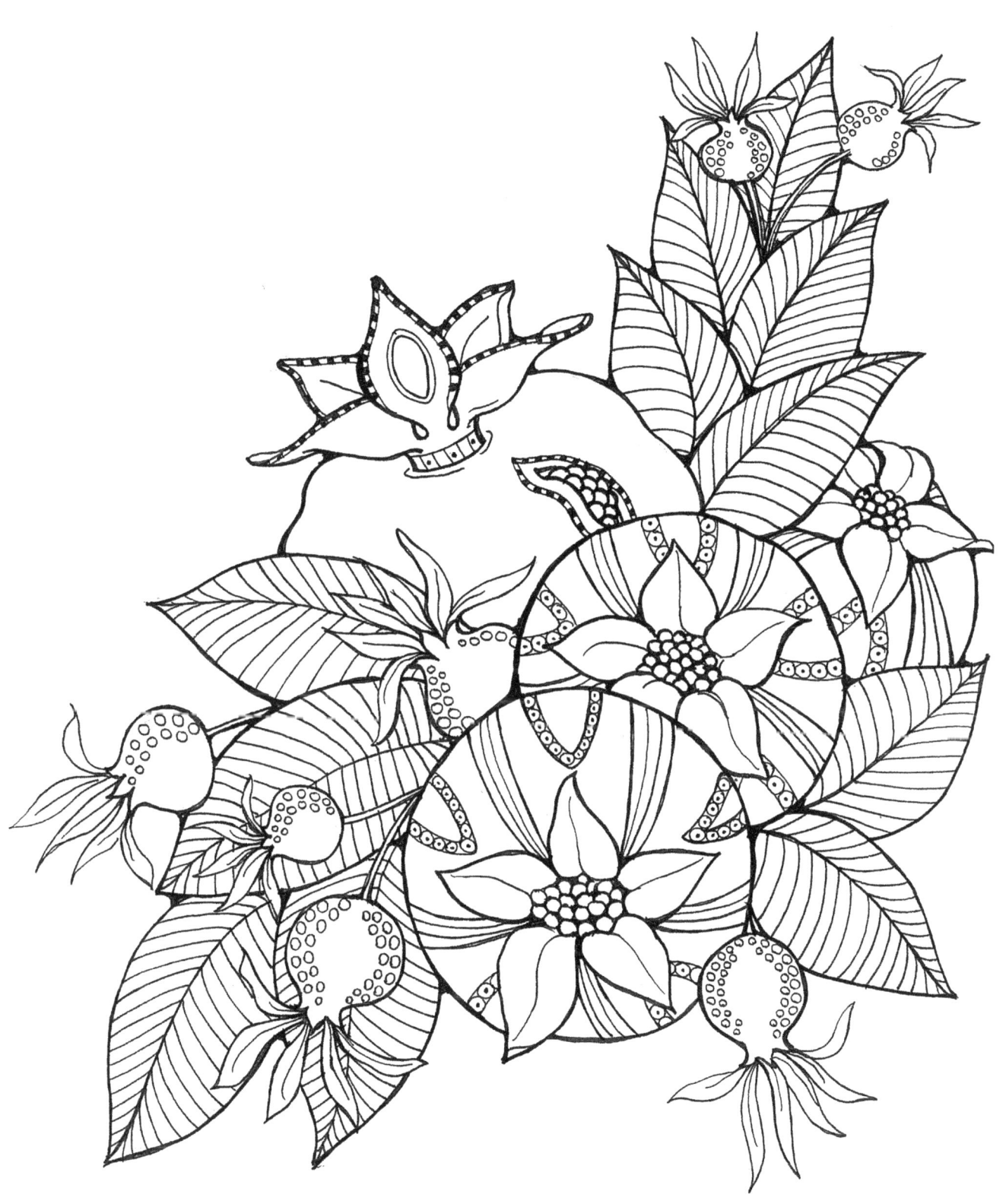

ILLUSTRATION 32

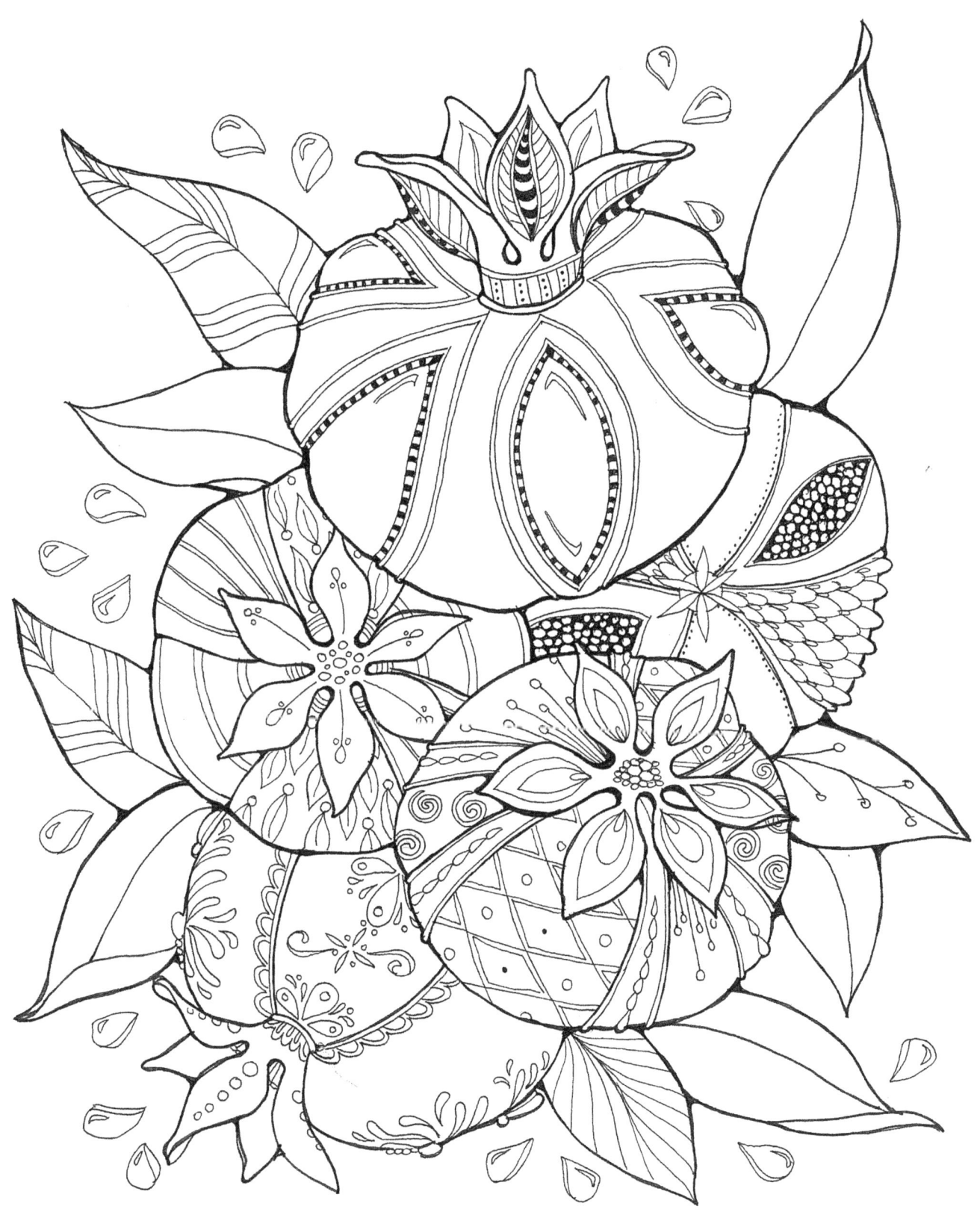

ILLUSTRATION 33

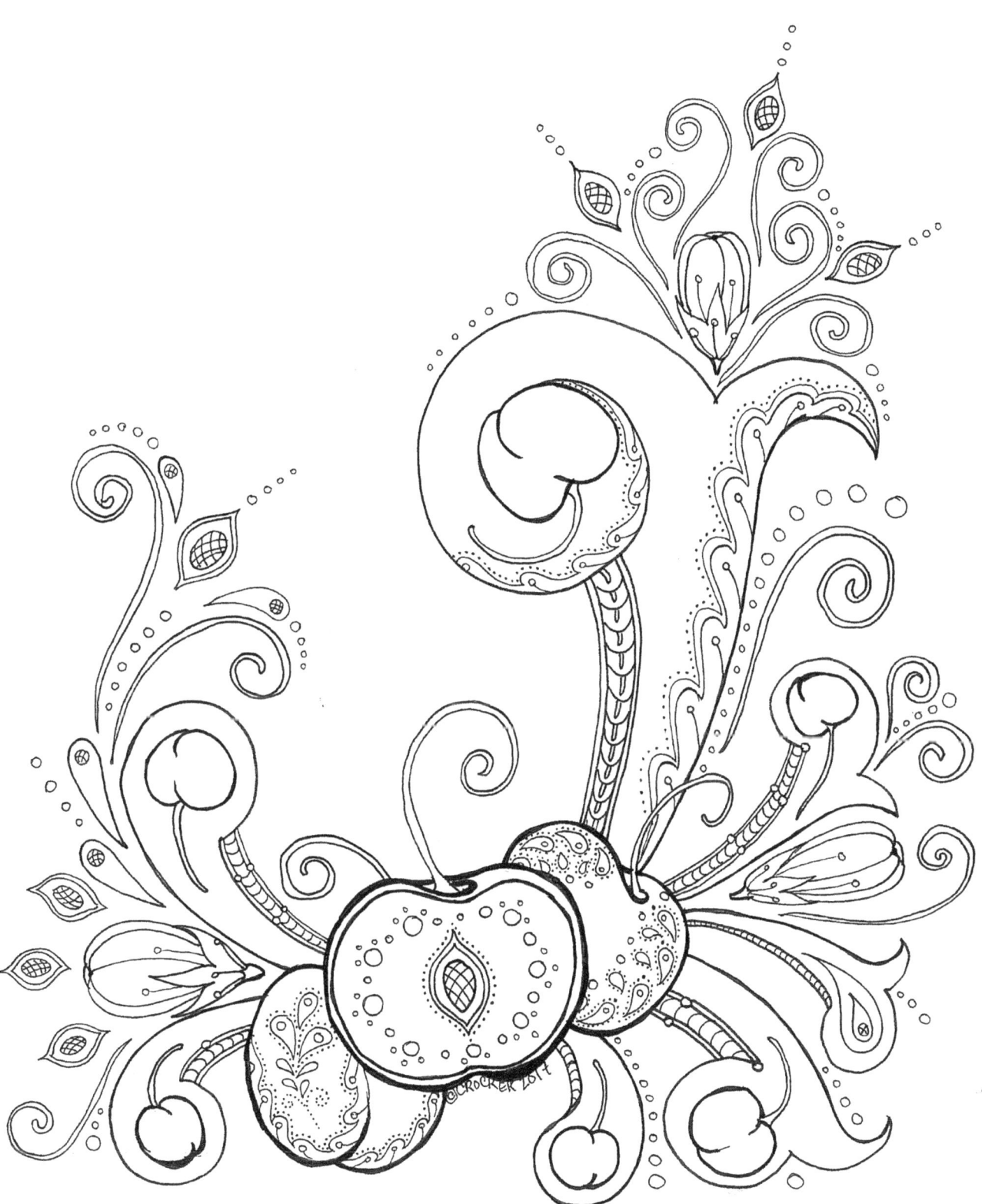

ILLUSTRATION 34

ILLUSTRATION 35

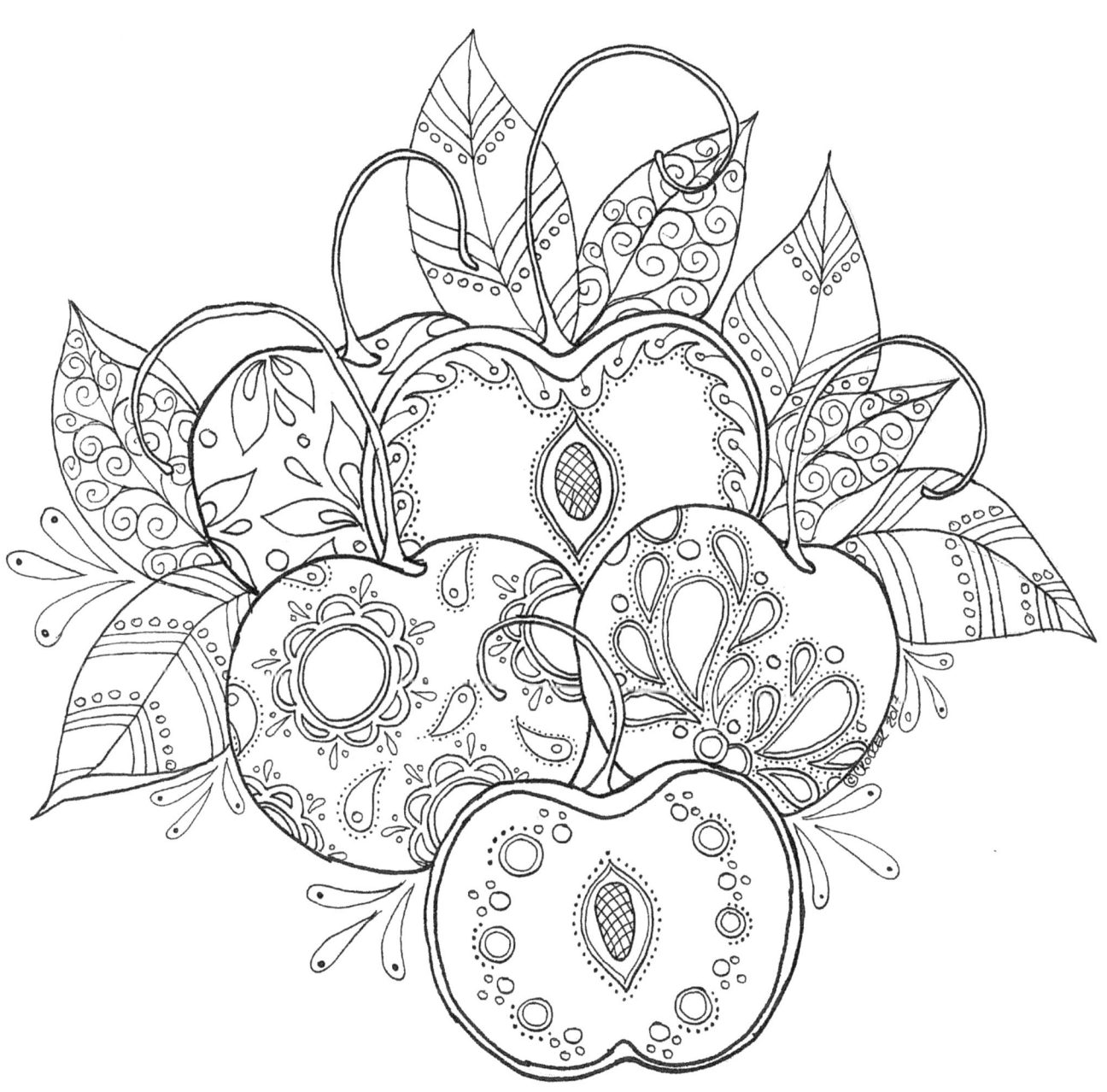

ILLUSTRATION 36

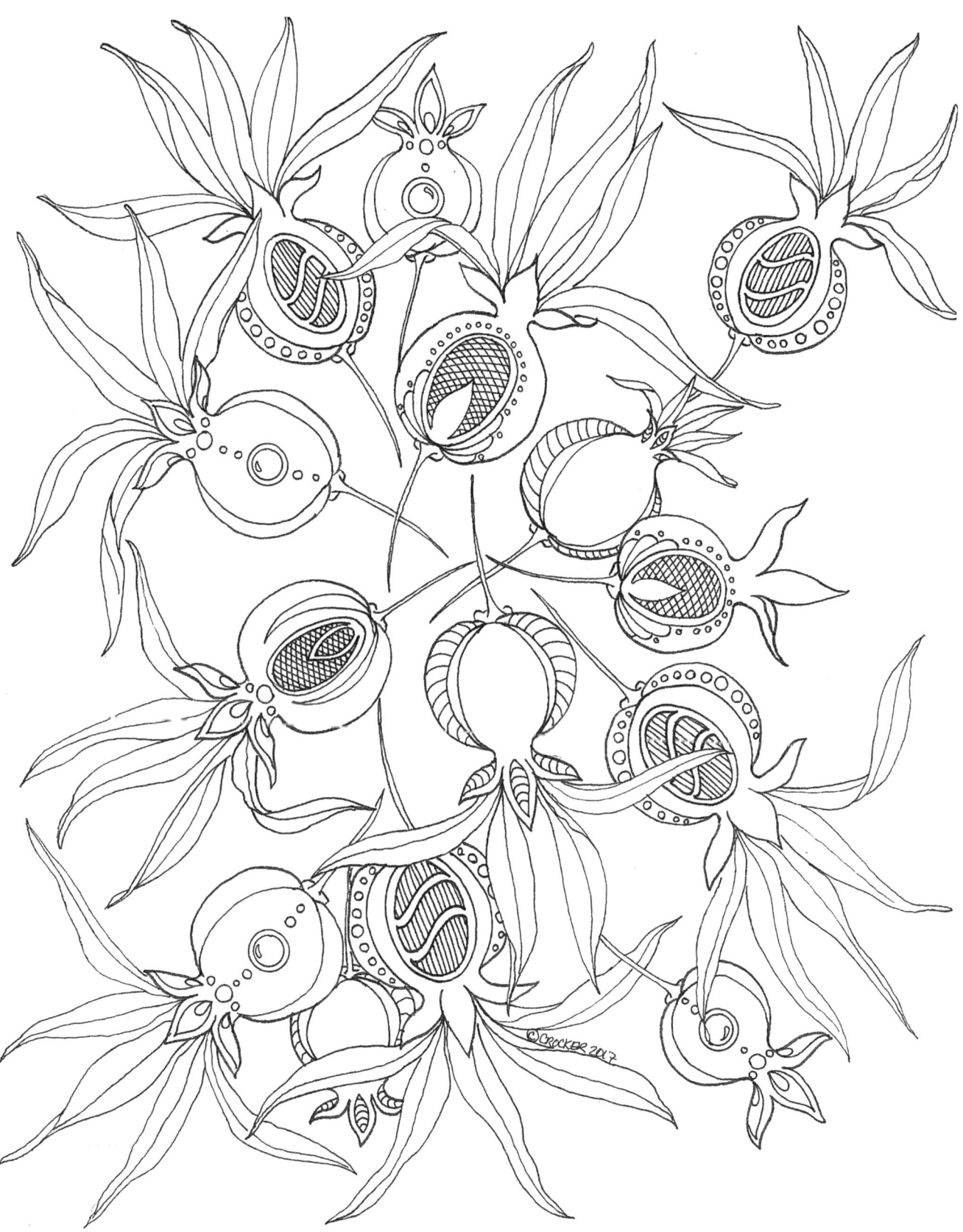

ILLUSTRATION 37

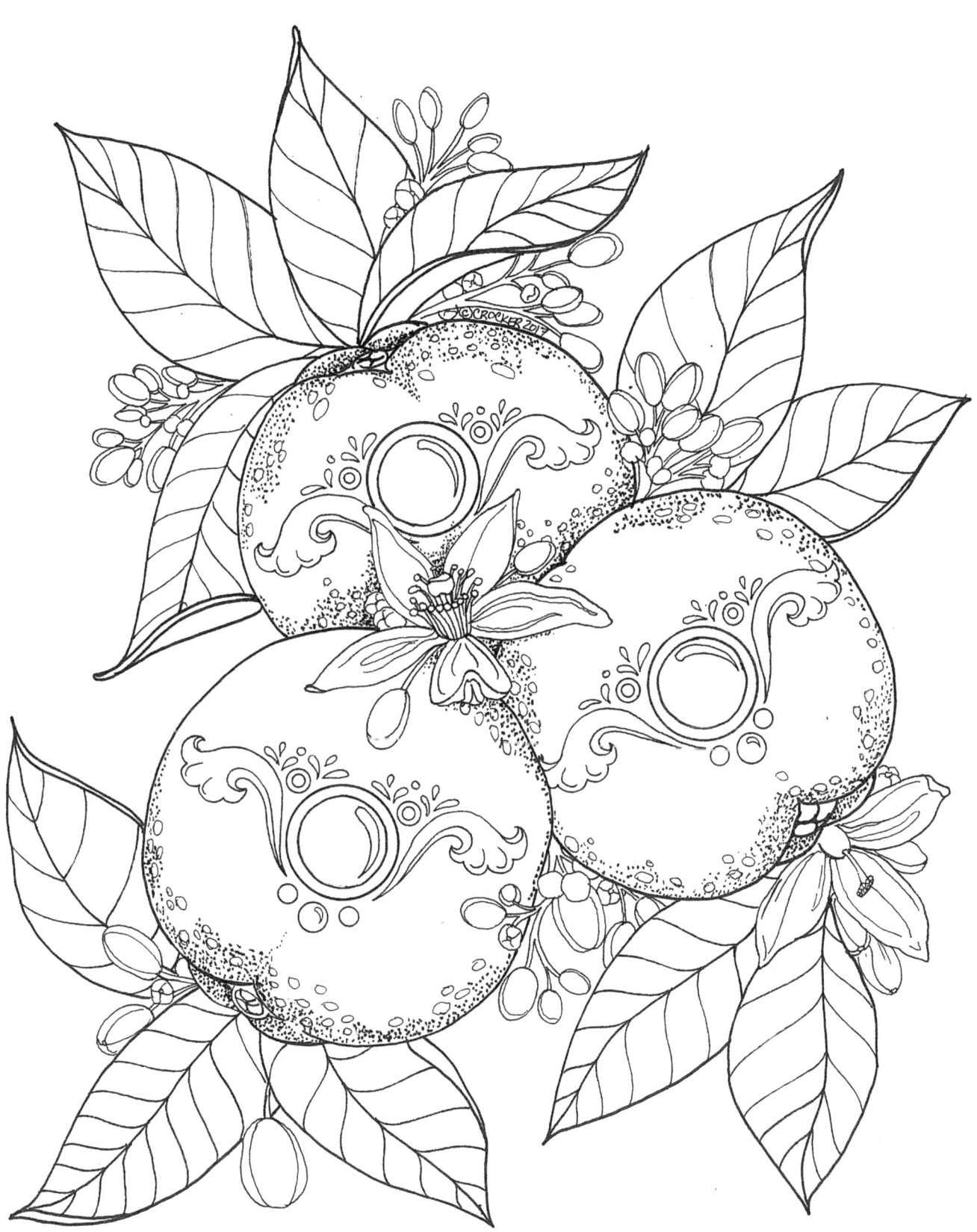

ILLUSTRATION 38

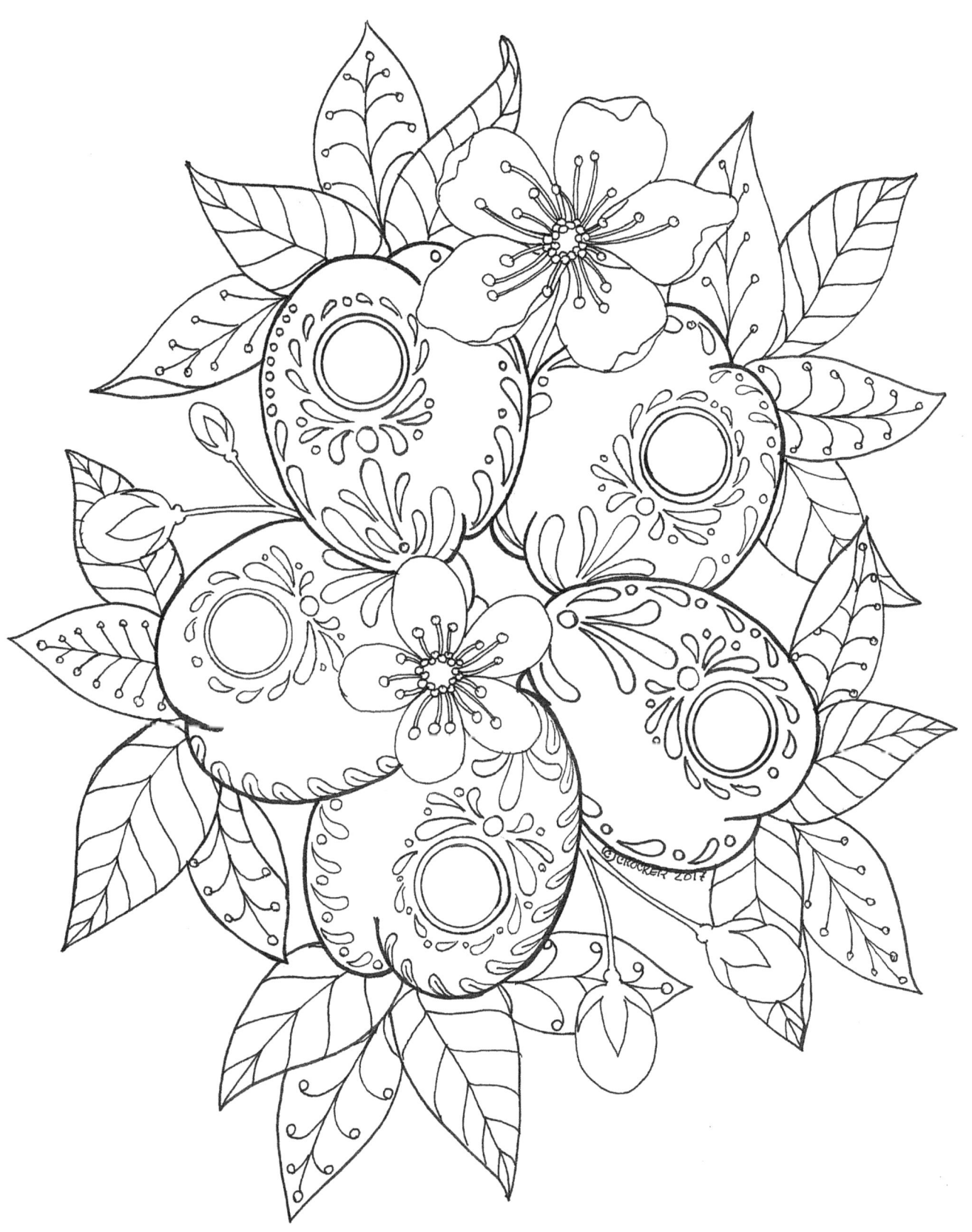

ILLUSTRATION 39

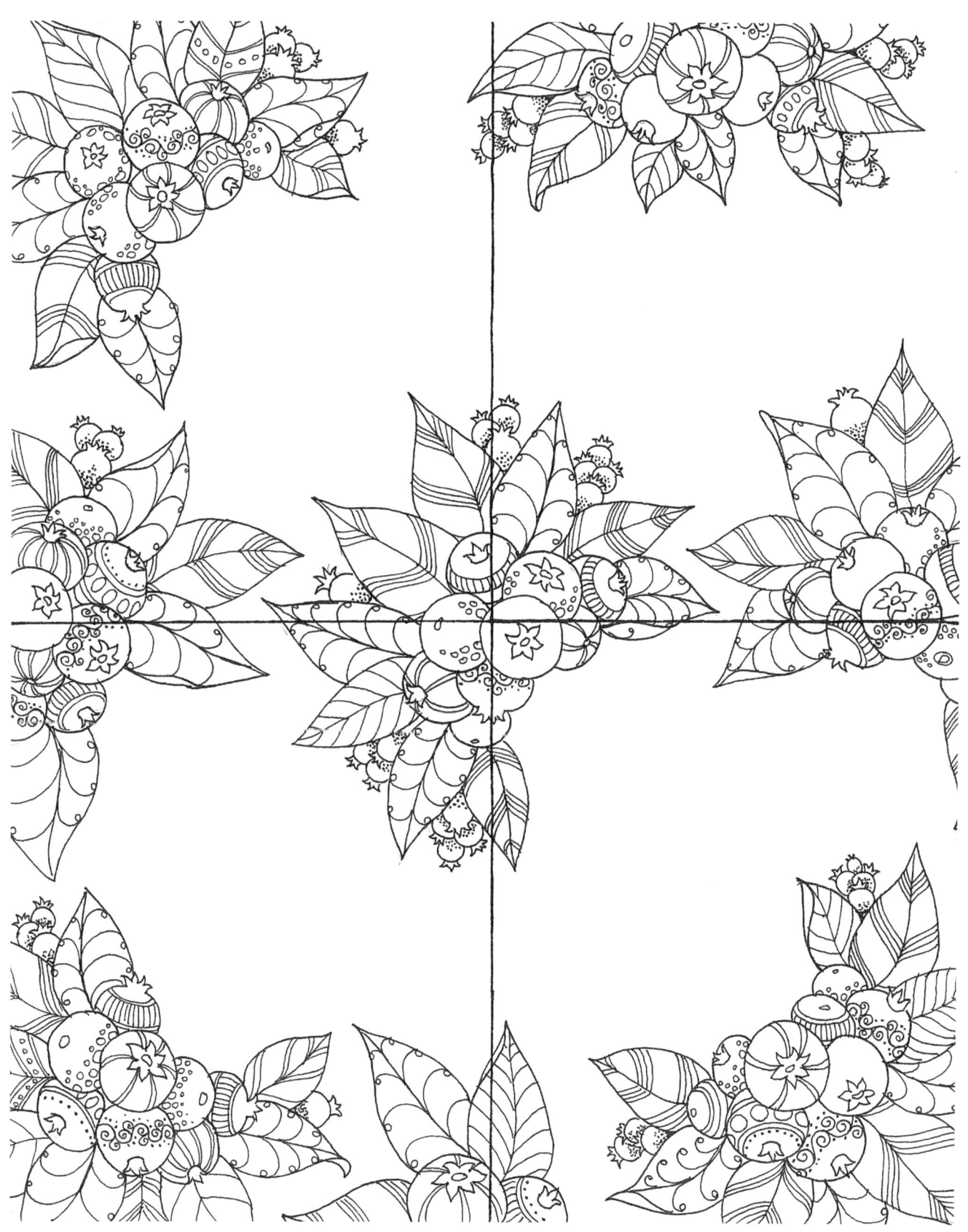

ILLUSTRATION 40

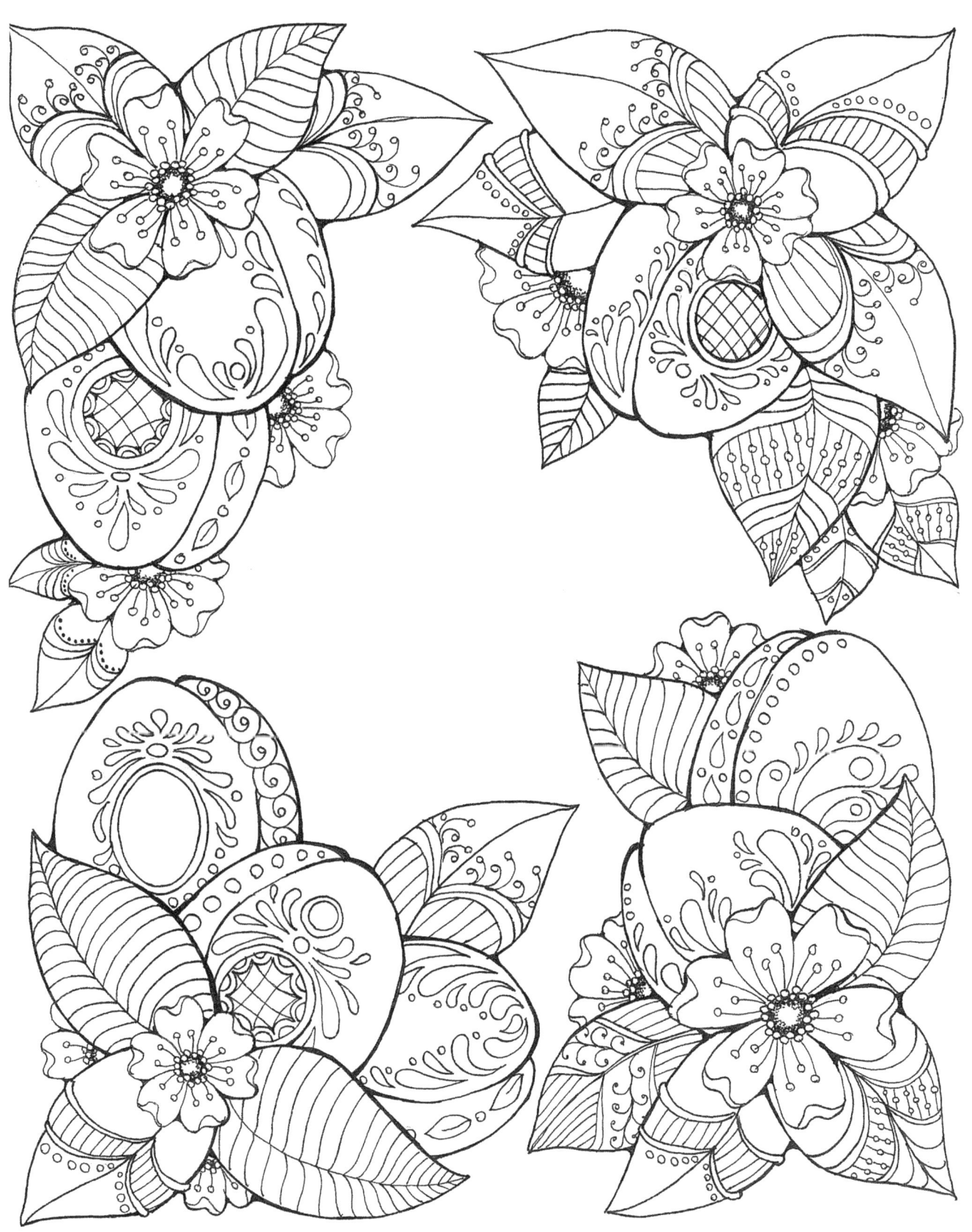

ILLUSTRATION 41

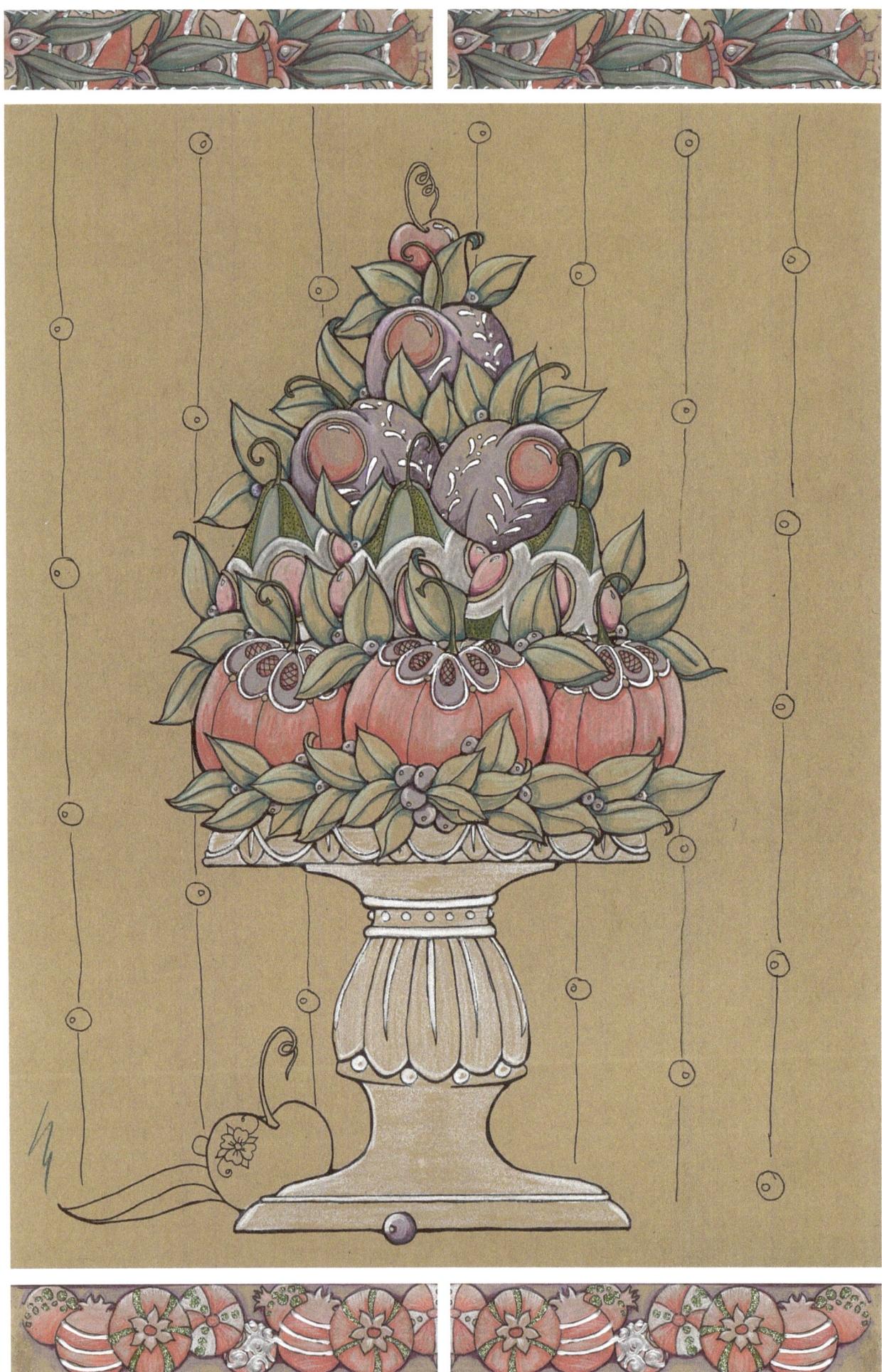

www.ingramcontent.com/pod-product-compliance
Lightning Source LLC
Chambersburg PA
CBHW051157220526

45473CB00003B/802